MOUNTSORREL

And its Associated Quarry Railways

By Ian P. Peaty

Mountsorrel Quarry crushing and sieving plant shrouded in dust in the 1930s with Peckett & Sons DORIS, built in 1928,and one of the 700 Company's private owner wagons.

Irwell Press Ltd.

Stoney Stanton Quarry in 1920 with a Hunslet 0-4-0ST shunting internal user only wagons with dumb buffers. A vertical boiler crane is in a deep pit behind.

BIBLIOGRAPHY

Enderby in 1881, A Snapshot of a Village, Sylvia Watton, 2001
Industrial Railways & Locos of Leicestershire and Rutland, Preliminary Handbook, Industrial Railway Society, A.R.Etherington and I.R.B.Bendall, 2006
A Short Account of Mountsorrel & the working of its Granite Quarry, The Building News 1870
Leicester Mercury Newpaper.
The Diaries of W.F.Martin (unpublished), 1896 to 1898.
The Canals of the East Midlands, Charles Hatfield, 1966
The Leicester Line, Philip A.Stevens, 1972
Ellis of Leicester, A Quaker Family's Vocation, Andrew Moore, 2003
Old Huncote, Michael Tanner, 1976
Reflections in Croft, Colin Cross, 1962
Geology of Leicestershire, N.J.Harrison, 1877
The Cliffe Hill Railway (Revised by D.H.Smith), M.H.Billington, 1997
The Leicester & Swannington Railway, C.R.Clinker, 1977

First published in the United Kingdom in 2012
by Irwell Press Limited, 59A, High Street, Clophill,
Bedfordshire MK45 4BE
Printed by Newnorth

Contents

GW00383866

Acknowledgements

I should like to record my grateful thanks to the following employees of Lafarge, for their assistance and the use of their photographs: Mark McClusky, Kim Shaw (see *Extracts from the Diaries of W.F. Martin, 1896-1898* from the Lafarge Aggregates Archive), Roy Newport and his 'railway team' at Barrow-on-Soar; Ian Brown and John Carpenter who have again most generously given invaluable information and permission to use their photographs. Former employees John Edwards, John Close and Chris Robson's contributions have been invaluable and very much appreciated.

Special thanks are given to David W. Webb for his most generous permission to use his photographs and for allowing me to draw upon his knowledge of Leicestershire railways. Likewise Andrew Moore, Alison Jackson and Sydney Leleux have loaned photographs while John Sloan and Noel Wakeling have been most helpful with local history. My thanks are expressed to Alison and Matt Alexander for their regular technical help.

The Staff at Leicester and Rutland Record Office have given me much assistance and have responded to my several requests for information. Richards Engineering Ltd of Leicester have kindly given me the use of several of their archive photographs which is much appreciated. My thanks are extended to the staff at the *Ely Herald* for their assistance, and to Archant Cambs 24 for permission to use their photographs of the Ely railway accident. Finally, as many of the photographs illustrated are of some considerable age, quality has sometimes suffered, but they have been included because of their historical importance. It has not been possible to identify all the photographers despite every reasonable attempt at locating them; my apologies should I have inadvertently omitted anyone.

All other photographs and plans not credited to the photographers whose most kind permission to publish their works is gratefully acknowledged, are those of the author.

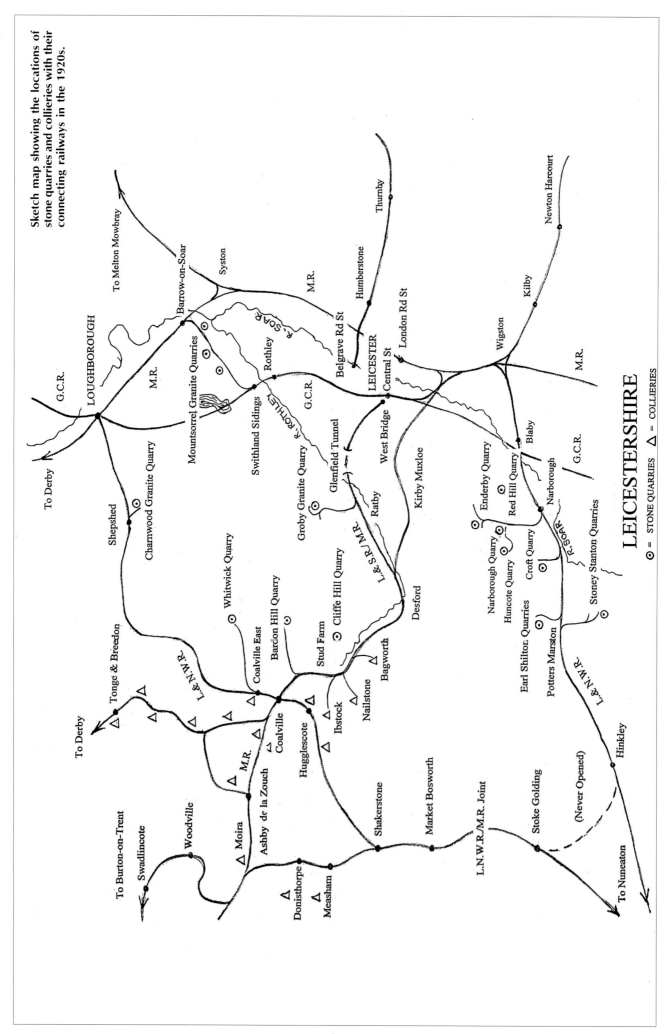

Sketch map showing the locations of stone quarries and collieries with their connecting railways in the 1920s.

LEICESTERSHIRE

⊙ = STONE QUARRIES △ = COLLIERIES

1. Introduction

The geology of Leicestershire is dominated by the igneous rocks which form the beautiful Charnwood Forest, immediately to the west of Leicester city. The eastern boundary is formed by the river Soar and its navigation on a north-south line. Running in this river valley is the former Midland Railway four track main line to Derby and Nottingham. To the east are the Lower Lias beds which reach a depth of over nine hundred feet and have been actively worked for over a hundred years. This activity is now conducted underground and the modern works, producing plaster products, are at Barrow-on-Soar, opposite the railway sidings of the Lafarge granite stone loading terminal.

To the west, at Coalville, coal has been extracted in and around the appropriately named town. The renowned Snibston Mine is now a museum under the management of the Leicestershire Museum Service. Other collieries were at Whitwick, where there was also a granite quarry, and a few miles south there were Ellistown, Ibstock, Desford, Nailstone and Measham Collieries; further west was the well known Moira Colliery near Burton-on-Trent. The east-west extent of the granite area is eight miles and north-south it extends for some sixteen miles. At the northern extremity was the Shepshed quarry while the southern-most quarrying took place at Stoney Stanton and Narborough, bounded by the old South Leicester line of the LNWR.

All the coal collieries and the granite quarries of any size were once served by railways; many of the quarries had their own railway networks, complete with a wonderful range of locomotives and private owner wagons, employing several different gauges. Today the largest granite quarry in Europe, Mountsorrel, lies on the north-eastern boundary; it still has a considerable private railway system in the ownership of the giant French aggregates business Lafarge Aggregates. On the western and southern areas, another firm, Aggregates Industries, have smaller railways, at Bardon Hill and Croft Quarries. Close to the coal measures is Stud Farm rail ballast loading plant; formerly owned by Tarmac Ltd, a narrow gauge railway connected it to the quarry at Markfield.

Quarries originally connected to the main line but now closed, include Charnwood Granite Co. at Shepshed, some four miles due west of Loughborough, the previously mentioned Whitwick Quarry and, to the west of Leicester city, the Groby Granite Co Ltd. These three quarries were in

A run-past on the Great Central Railway of the recently restored Mountsorrel Granite Company open wagons, near Rothley in 2010, hauled by a preserved class 31 diesel and hopefully the precursor to steam freight trains. John Sloan.

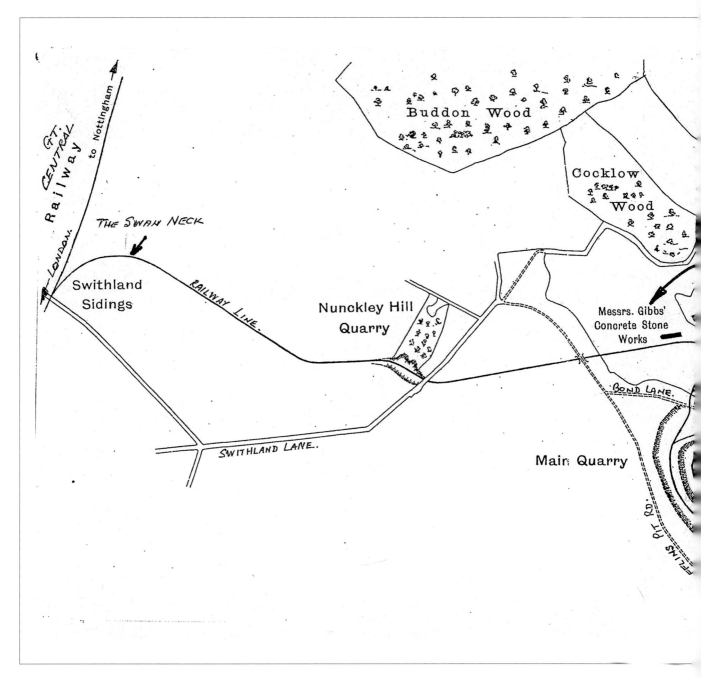

the ownership of Amalgamated Roadstone Corporation Ltd. (ARC). Other quarries, some now closed but which once had railway systems, are included in this book because of their relationship with Redland Aggregates Ltd. Quarries acquired in 1977 by Lafarge Aggregates included Mountsorrel, Enderby and Stoney Stanton, Narborough, Red Hill and Huncote and Earl Shilton. Mountsorrel remains the last within this group that is fully active, with an enviable pedigree in producing the vital aggregates for industry. More than half its production is transported by rail.

Development of the local collieries and connection to the major market of Leicester, was first enabled by the construction of the Leicester & Swannington Railway, opening for traffic on Tuesday 17th July 1832. On this same day, Lord Stamford's Groby Quarry and the Whitwick Colliery were connected to the new line, coal traffic commencing on 22nd April 1833 with Bagworth and Ibstock soon following. Both the LNWR and MR inevitably became keen competitors for this growing traffic but surprisingly they collaborated in two jointly operated lines. An Act of 1867 for the Ashby & Nuneaton Joint Railway, included a committee of three directors from each company, E.S. Ellis of Leicester representing the MR. His brother John Ellis had been one of the moving forces behind the Leicester & Swannington. The northern end of this line joined the Leicester to Burton line at Moira, with a junction midway at Shakerstone which joined the MR line to Coalville. At the southern end, the line joined the South Leicester line of the LNWR and further east, on the outskirts of Leicester, the second joint line left Narborough station on a short mineral branch built in 1890. This was constructed expressly for the Enderby quarries. A similar mineral branch was built in 1860 by the Midland Railway, from Barrow-on-Soar to the Mountsorrel Quarry.

The story of granite extraction in Leicestershire is dominated by the major titled landowners, Lord Lanesborough, Lord Maynard and the Earl of Stamford & Warrington. However, the tale would not be complete without the inclusion of the lesser landowners such as the Ellis, Everard, Rawson, Martin, Marston and Freer families.

As noted, the Mountsorrel granite quarry is Europe's largest ; today the aggregates industry employs 20,000 people working in some 1,300 quarries in the UK, worth some £3 billion a year. In 1900, production of granite for all uses was 2½ million tons, of which Leicestershire produced one million tons. The Lafarge Aggregates group employs now 750 people in Leicestershire at twelve sites, with 400 staff at Syston, the UK headquarters. At the Mountsorrel quarry there are over 100 employees engaged in all

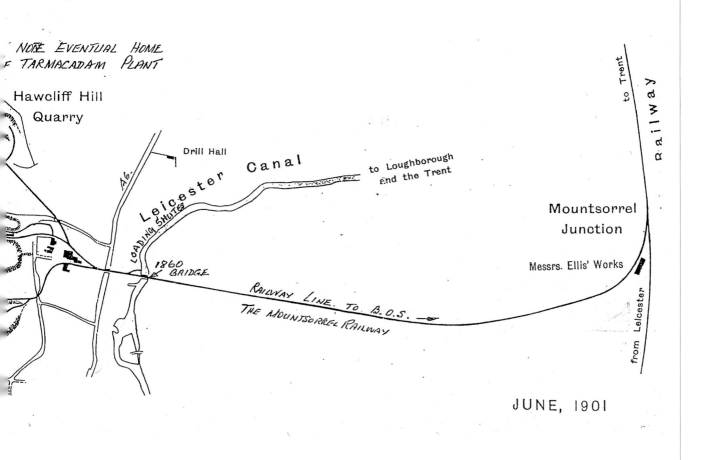

SKETCH PLAN OF MOUNTSORREL QUARRIES
WITH RAILWAY AND CANAL CONNECTIONS

SCALE 6INS to 1 MILE

NOTE EVENTUAL HOME OF TARMACADAM PLANT

Hawcliff Hill Quarry

Drill Hall

A6.

Leicester Canal

LOADING SHUTES

1860 BRIDGE

to Loughborough and the Trent

Mountsorrel Junction

Messrs. Ellis' Works

to Trent

Railway

from Leicester

RAILWAY LINE TO B.O.S.

THE MOUNTSORREL RAILWAY

JUNE, 1901

MOUNTSORREL RAILWAY

NO ROAD

TRESPASSERS WILL

BE PROSECUTED.

An original enamel sign of 1900 dissuading young trespassers from damaging wagons at the isolated quarries on the western branch to Swithland Sidings. Bob Withers.

aspects of the extractive industry, from surveyors, drivers, engineers, laboratory technicians, weighbridge operators and explosive experts, to sales and administrative staff.

Over a third of UK demand for aggregate is in the South East, and this is where the greater percentage of production is taken, by rail. Mountsorrel's annual production is currently around 260 million tonnes, of which half is sent out by rail from the Barrow-on-Soar terminal. Twelve of the company's depots handle the local road distribution from these rail terminals. Other locations supplied by rail include Network Rail depots at Crewe and Doncaster.

Top. A 'home made' compressor to power rock drills in the quarry, built at the Company's workshops in the 1920s. It sits on an old dumb buffered open wagon chassis. Lafarge Aggregates.

Right. A caterpillar tracked shovel working at a quarry face in 1930 after a recent blasting has brought down the stone, ready for loading up in rail wagons to be taken to the crusher.

Left. This vertical boiler rail mounted crane with swivel action was built in 1912 by the Bramley Engineering Co Ltd of Leeds. The absence of weather and safety protection was normal for the period.

Below. Mountsorrel Railway bridge of 1860 over the Leicester Navigation, looking east in 1920. The stone chute for loading canal boats is on the right.

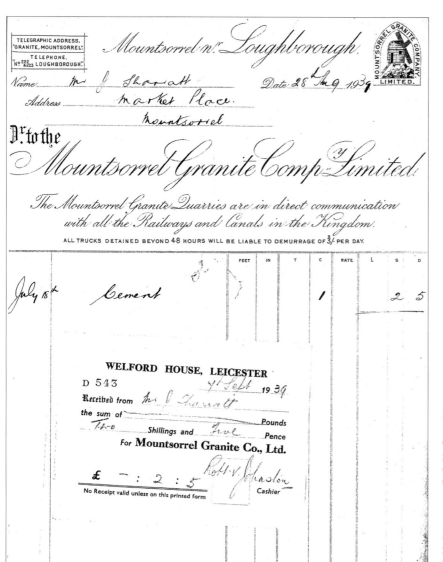

Mountsorrel nr Loughborough

MOUNTSORREL GRANITE COMPANY LIMITED.

Name _Mr J Sharratt_   Date _28 Aug 1939_

Address _Market Place._

Mountsorrel

Dr to the

Mountsorrel Granite Company Limited

The Mountsorrel Granite Quarries are in direct communication with all the Railways and Canals in the Kingdom.

ALL TRUCKS DETAINED BEYOND 48 HOURS WILL BE LIABLE TO DEMURRAGE OF 3/- PER DAY.

	FEET	IN	T	C	RATE	L	S	D
July 18th Cement				1			2	5

WELFORD HOUSE, LEICESTER

D 543   _4th Sept_ 19 39

Received from _Mr J Sharratt_

the sum of _Two_ ————————— Pounds

Two Shillings and _Five_ Pence

For **Mountsorrel Granite Co., Ltd.**

£ — : 2 : 5   _Robt V Johnston_

No Receipt valid unless on this printed form   Cashier

Left. Mountsorrel Granite Company Ltd letterhead used in the 1930s, which displayed the windmill logo. Notice is given that the quarries are in direct communication with all the Railways and Canals in the Kingdom.

Below. Enderby Quarry with its narrow gauge system being worked by the German loco CHESHAM and to the left Bagnall saddle tank LESTER.

2. Mountsorrel and Stoney Stanton Quarries

Extracts from the diaries of W.F.Martin, 1896 to 1898.

These diaries were written by twenty year old W.F. Martin, who was born in 1876 and died in action at Ypres in 1915. The diaries indicate the enthusiasm that he had for training in the local Leicestershire Yeomanry, regularly practising 'pegging' with a lance on horseback, and for shooting. As might be expected, given his well-to-do background in this part of Leicestershire, he took an active part in riding with the hounds of the Quorn Hunt. He also made many forays into the countryside with game shoots. His job took him all over, especially at the busy time of the construction of the Great Central Railway and the building of the Mountsorrel Railway connection from the quarry to the west, connecting with the Swithland Sidings on the GCR. These exchange sidings were used by the contractor for this stretch of the GCR, Henry Lovatt who purchased large quantities of aggregate from the Mountsorrel Quarry. Martin's job entailed considerable measuring-up of land and taking levels with the drawing of appropriate plans and details and setting-out of bridges and sidings. He also undertook a supervisory role in almost all spheres of the quarry. They are very much working notes and at some points the precise meaning is difficult to fathom but they give an unusual insight into the hurly-burly of construction life back then, cheerfully uninhibited by much in the way of health, safety or any other considerations! He was grandson to William John Martin who acquired the small business in 1850 from a Mr Jackson.

His diaries include several sketches and various technical terms. Daily weather reports are given as well as his social activities, such as sporting events and boating on the river Soar. His father, Robert F. Martin, senior director of the Mountsorrel Granite Co Ltd is referred to as RFM; all close associates are in fact noted by their initials. Notwithstanding this, the steam locomotives are all given their full names, and it is apparent that many trips were taken on the footplate, especially down to the Swithland junction on the GCR, and not always strictly for business purposes.

There is considerable comment on many horses, including hunters and quarry work horses, including costs of feeding, health condition and prices paid. Numerous trips were taken on horseback and train to the quarries at Stoney Stanton, sometimes with his father, as developments were taking place there. Stoppages due to bad weather and many break-downs with the crushing mill plant is dutifully recorded, with replacement parts ordered, and comments regarding the adjustment of depths between rollers on the crushing plant. Regular visits were made to the Company's hospital at Mountsorrel, visiting patients and the doctor in charge and conducting the business there.

DIARY 1896

1st June. X stock taken, about 36 wagons. Prepared box for bones[1] to go to Cambridge.

2nd June. When there is not rough to be loaded the men shift rammel[2] at ¾ a day. Persuaded Freer to remove the bones from the board room. Arrival of Warner, the Midland[3] man 11a.m. much roasted and promised to do his best about dirty wagons, at putting down extra length of siding to open up junction. Engine up line to Nunkley Hill with RFM.

5th June. Found Brown and another loading up a Midland wagon with refuse and told them to ram it down tight. $^5/_8$ inch web rather narrow for our rails. Working stress at 4 or 5 tons to the inch = area of bottom flange in inches. A = p/f.

6th June. Started to set out Nunkley Hill bridge.

8th June. Viewed permanent way on new line before breakfast. Timber up Airds[7] tramway with Wilkie.

10th June. Ballast ordered down into yard with no instructions what they were to be filled with. Mr Baker supposed to know but naturally did not! Is it chips or top stone? It is a muddling way of doing things not to send a written order.

11th June. Went up after lunch, met young Lovett far side Nunkley Hill. Found Goodenough baring rock at far side of cutting. The bridge is nicked out on the road. Showed young Lovett round quarry and 'tead' him. *Kathleen* burst a tube in morning.

12th June. Irons had a shot blown off in the Hawcliffe which blew a mill wagon off its wheels, being too near it when fired. Bridge on common should be begun today. The permanent way from 54ch. to Nunkley Hill must have its ballast properly cleaned. The question of dirty wagons is just as bad as ever, the arrangement about platelayers having apparently ceased to act. The fact being they find they have not strength enough to do the job as quickly as required so they find they are referring to Derby for orders and doing nothing meanwhile.

13th June. Concreting of bridge on Common begun, left off about 8am and wallers back to Sheffield for Sunday. Arrangement about chips. All in Lovatt's wagons[4] to go for the main line, all in our side tips for our Branch and to be charged accordingly.

15th June. The ganger of platelayers is Cheshire and Burton the lad will be a ganger some day if he does well. Went down to Swithland junction to measure the excess that Lovatt has covered over the specified ground in the plan. Mr Baker caught a wagon going to Lovatts about half full of chips and sent it back to the Mills, reprimanded Warner, as Stuart has complained about that already. They have the foundations out of Swithland bridge at last. Made tracing of the excess ground bagged by Stuart, 700 sq.yds.

16th June. Found out what information I could about dirty wagons. Met RFM at Barrow to go to Derby 10.45, arrive 11.45. Went to see Briddon re. dirty wagons and Turner's head clerk, re. improvement at junction. After lunch to a private wagon owners association meeting.

17th June. Told J. Crooks to give in an account each day of what Midland wagons he has to clean, exclusive of course of those unloaded in the wharf. Great argument with G. Baker as to whether main line permanent way is to be 10 inches low under Hawcliffe bridge or not; almost came to blows. No bridge rails ordered, Sidney has ordered them this afternoon. 4.45 arrival of G. Baker in a great stew to announce that 4 of Lovatt's wagons had been sent up the line full of bottom ballast, would I find out if they were for the main line or our branch or what? I failed to find out as there was no one about owing to the rain. In future we are going to send out no stuff without a written order so as to avoid the hopeless confusion which would otherwise be inevitable. Ran some quoins[5] up in a mill wagon to the bridge on the Common, got the men in hot water for not leaving them in the siding.

19th June. GB took them up on *Willie* after breakfast. GB has a story that the walking ganger told him they had already ballasted the line from Nottingham to the reservoir with slag. That is rot as there is no permanent way or anything like it down near Quorn. Order from Logan and H for 1 truck of randoms which looks better, the Notts; people ought to keep them to a bargain. Letter from Turner to say he has ordered alteration at junction to be proceeded with. Inspected Bowes steam navvy.

20th June. Baker found masons on common not filling up space between masonry and muck in counterforts on common, so stopped them at that part of the job altogether. Got the top of Hawcliffe bridge after much trouble and smashing and nearly upsetting the 3 ton crane down on the permanent way. Also knocking off about 3 corbel stones.

7th July. *Mills* not running, boilers being scoured today and yesterday. Steam to be got up this afternoon. The siding down at the junction has been altered now for about a fortnight.

8th July. Up the line 11.30, found points rod smashed and the guard swore they hadn't done it. Also chair broken.

17th July. Baker went to SS[10] saw the LNW man who said don't go bothering among these local agents when short of wagons but go straight to Euston. The LNW are not giving us wagons enough and also will not clear out our junction, often bringing in a load of supplies and going away again light.

21st July. 200 tons were ordered by Hall and again sent off on the same day. The Midland will begin to get agitated if that kind of thing goes on.

23rd July. 11.30am Smith & Johnson from Midland and LNW to see about 22cwt to the ton, they hadn't the ghost of a case. 5pm *Robbie* bent a side rod through a bit of rough tumbling off, stayed and saw it straightened.

29th July. A barge horse[6] feeding close by the basin somehow backed in and was drowned or choked in the mud which apparently is about 6ft deep, though it don't look it. They dragged it up the canal to somewhere near the mill and pulled it out there.

5th Aug. Out 7am. Saw timber unloaded and measured one Quebec elm, the rest Norway. When timber comes on two wagons with a third to take the projection, does the MR[3] charge for the third one?

A 'Blondin' aerial ropeway bucket system commonly used to bring stone from deep quarries to the surface.

6th Aug. Up to the two bridges. The permanent way was never put down as proposed last Thursday and there is no reason why it should be yet because if it is there will not be room to put up a scaffold between it and the abutment (so Bromhead says but if it was done on the Common why not at Nunkley Hill?). Found the points at the bottom end of the loop lying so that a runaway would go down into the yard, changed them over. Also loaded wagons on both lines which is contrary to regulations. The coping of the last bit of wall in Bond Lane is just about finished so there is nothing to prevent the top being tipped. There is a pair of points put in and a tip being started in the field above Harris' house now that the timber has come and is cut up into sleepers. There are as yet no runaway points this side of BL (Bond Lane?) bridge which there ought to be.

7th Aug. Stones loaded up for Aberdeen. To Stanton ordered waterproof sheet at Fosters. Looked at Lanes Hill where the rock is much better. Bowes cannot raise 10 trucks a day of bottom ballast now but sends his train every two days.

12th Aug. On to Hawcliffe. Six wagons being loaded with Lovatt's stuff, high level line. Lovatts are taking 35 a day now. Saw wagon 48, tipped into mill with some very big rough indeed.

15th Aug. Saw the two bridges, Baker passed the tarring of the counterforts last night. Permanent way wants seeing to badly all through the line. Found one or two sleepers under pinned with 1 or 2 bits of drain pipe. Extra from Lovatts 1.2.0 Removal of earth from farm land

at base of stone near Bond Lane. 1 man 40 hours at 6d per hour plus supervision. 1300 tons of 3 x 6 stock just cleared out SS.

20th Aug. Saw Stuart and dinner with WJM Directors had tea in my rooms. Whaite back to work on *Willie*.

21st Aug. Fine. Up to bridge on Common. Into quarry. Steam is being got up in the old 3 ton crane. The big stone was got down with a jack and is to be shot with a 3-6" hole. Talked to Bardiner about drills and their price.

24th Aug. Irons is putting out some rough for Dawes which is far too good, made him pick best out for pitchings for Lovatt, about 200 tons ordered, 6s ton.

25th Aug. Took engine and out to Airds. Smith has a temporary job out there sharpening tools. Machine drillers drill day work and get their drills as they want them. Lovatt's loaders 3s 4d per day. Stumpers 3d per day, another stumping gang has just been put on. Saw a man getting on an absolutely bare face with nothing to hold to but his rope.

28th Aug. To SS. At Lanes Hill the rock is nothing just now but mush. Bowes ought to push the railway through at the narrow place, leaving the mush on the left as steep as it will stand, get into his quarry, clean it out to Lovatts, work away the sound rock and get in behind the mush on the left.

29th Aug. About 40 wagons up to Lovatts.

7th Sept. Talk to GB who has been having trouble with WB at SS re. engine taking no notice of signal at junction.

12th Sept. Found Woodhouse working with Robbie because *Willie* in with broken exhaust pipe. GB went up branch saw Lovatts loading muck from their heap, then comes a letter complaining that the bottom ballast we are sending them is very dirty, that Stuart will take it up again at our cost.

14th Sept. Found Bishop scratching slate off the tubes in *Willie's* boiler which is being kept open for the inspector to see, being in a bad way. RWLD says that we have got Lovatts so on toast that if they don't buy 100,000 tons in all they will have to pay 6d per ton extra on all ballast and 3d on chips because we gave them a reduced price on condition of their buying 100,000 tons. 4.30 Enter Grasby and Ellis[8] wanting 4 side trucks rammel to pitch up line just above BLB. Up and gave orders to Peters at once. Wagons were put up that evening. While our folks were shunting a wagon on straight road in yard quite slowly the axle box broke in two and the wagon continued to run with the journal against the spring. Put it on the siding very carefully and without accident 5.45pm. Up to hospital then on home, wind bad for cycling.

16th Sept. To Sorrel 10.15, Boiler inspector over yesterday. Spur wheels from Abels. Steel from Halls. Exhaust pipe for *Willie*.

19th Sept. Warrener – application from him to lengthen siding, went in to Turner August 8th so no harm to write and stir Turner up. Maintenance still under discussion, meanwhile we are to do nothing and not pay anything.

23rd Sept. When going down Airds with Walter they got off the road and cut up about two rail lengths because *Sutton* did not stop at once. 4.30 Enter Prance to say his cylinder, low pressure, weight 4 tons, had cracked, if he brought it here on a cart could we load it up for him. Showed him round, gave him tea and put him up Airds as far as possible with *Robbie*. Met Facer who asked when the coal was coming in. The coal is here but the invoice from Mick has not come. Facer of course has his from the Babbington Co.

24th Sept. Some ballast wagons from MR up with a lot of brick bats in them. GB ordered that on no account were they to be cleaned but to be filled bats and all. No reply from Turner yet re. junction.

7th Oct. Saw 5 ton crane in which bottom nut is loose and many other things are wrong. Up to NH[9] with Sidney and Lovatt to settle where rock begins and ends. Jawed Lovatt very strongly about his runaway which occurred when I was away, 3 wagons slipped from *Aberdeen* and started down the incline, *Walter* happened to be coming down gently in front of them. R Baker has at last ordered a catch point. Whole thing spoilt by *Walter* coming down with us on board, ran down a train of empties below him in spite of my reminding it was wrong, he was backed by Sydney!! J. Lovatt noticed it all but said nothing at the time.

8th Oct. J Lovatt here at 10am started taking out earthworks quantities using cross sections he had made. Lovatts asked if they might store 20lbs dynamite in our magazine. Leave refused by G. Baker and RFM. Runaway point is in. Started Lovatt up line but stopped by work going on beyond Common bridge.

10th Oct. Top ballast supply has been temporarily stopped in consequence of a breakdown to one of Lovatt's engines.

21st Oct. Extra from Lovatts yesterday to putting in clean ballast and rubble drain, filled with the rest. To SS with RFM. Inspected Lanes Hill then round past Lovett's pit and Granitethorpe to Calver Hill. Bowes is to dig trial holes. Watched a tube put into *Kathleen* after 5.30.

28th Oct. Rod shifted from points by crane, the length of the Mason's shed, started this morning. Trains will run tomorrow over it.

30th Oct. Order for randoms and other things from MR. If tubes are ordered from Elliott instead of Hunslet we should save £18 on 2 tons (231 tubes) rolled seamless. To SS with RFM to see Grace re. sidings for the Enderby and SS. Grace says he wants them our side of the turnpike and that he will have a level crossing and a horse which means he won't want the partition down which is a good thing. We have lost St Pancras order, letter 2 days ago through bad stuff. They use xx rolls at SS about $2^3/_8$ centre, 13 teeth in the row and it makes good xx and bad x. A plug shot out in *Robbie* yesterday morning and caught Gamble in the leg inflicting fearful agony.

4th Nov. Rough loading with shovels in Clint Hill stopped. Rough sent off to MS two wagons as per order. Into Clint Hill bottom. To Cary Hill and Lanes Hill, Calver in afternoon. Roman remains coming up out of trial hole, earth been dug over before looks as if we have hit on fault or dyke to put trial hole in and Romans knew of it and put a well there.

6th Nov. Mills stopped and wires put up in engine house, watched shot in Cary Hill. It crumpled up about 20yds of railway and a wagon of squares blocks.

17th Nov. Returned by Midland train stopped at Elmsthorpe specially for us, had to buy new return ½.

18th Nov. *Kathleen* broke tubes this morning. 1 mill rope off and leathers put on, $^9/_{16}$in, another coming off dinner time so engine running with 6. Chairman over and trial of hose on mills from mills engine pump and loco hose.

23rd Nov. Found level crossings paved and many randoms over. Greasley promised to reload them and send them back. Watched the stays being taken out of *Kathleen* and the leathering and splicing of the mill ropes ($^9/_{16}$ths instead of $^1/_2$in).

25th Nov. Patch for *Kathleen* fire box as a place had worn to $^3/_8$ths.

8th Dec. Finished up 40ft of Calver Hill. Watched loading of engine for Holwell by boss and gang of men using our timber and jacks. They proposed starting at 1pm to get her unloaded by 3pm but when I left at 7pm the job was only half done.

9th Dec. Found engine still being loaded

with a new boss. Engine still loading at 3pm. New siding at junction nearly done.

14th Dec. Lovatt wagon in gullet came off rails with *Walter*. The little Waite would not bother to get it on properly but pulled on, consequence the wagon rolled over. Early in morning *Walter* had run right through the gate between the main quarry and the Hawcliffe owing to Waite forgetting to open it. Evening *Willie* running a tank into gullet, his draw bar broke and tank bumped in the same wagon again. Waite has been removed into the quarry under Peters. Down with Warners last train to junction to see addition, which is very useful as now they can swing through with a full train without fear of being stopped.

16th Dec. *Kathleen* burst one tube. 10.30am up line with RFM, GB SB and Willie to settle up finally (to be hoped) what yet remains to be done. Cutting sides are sliding all over the place, the pot holes are coming down hill.

17th Dec. *Kathleen* burst another tube and *Robbie* in with a broken spring bracket so the whole place about standing. 30 or 40 wagons in yard unable to get away to junction and Airds loco waiting at top for wagons and utterly unable to get any. After 5.30 all 4 engines out, the quarry to finish up, the mill yard to empty about 53 wagons to get to junction and empties up again, 4 wagons for Lovatts. Reached home 7.30 and when I left Sorrel all engines were in by *Kathleen* who over at the junction with the last train (17).

18th Dec. Out to Lanes Hill they have the gullet through and the line will be through tonight and a train loaded inside. We just caught the 4.10 as Shepherd kept it for us.

21st Dec. After lunch with WM and saw Johnson. Then took a day man and examined ditch where Airds crosses our line, also the rock there and found safe. One of Lovatt's wagons ran off the line and smashed gate between Hawcliffe and main quarry nearly hitting young Woodhouse. GB is to send back all wagons which are very unsafe. Grubbed up stone drain down NH branch and cut channel for the water to drain it off where it is overflowing the sleepers.

1897

5th Jan. Started per route engine *Frank* about 12am. Rugby viaduct over LNW is well worth seeing being three spans on rocking levers like the Forth bridge. Catesby tunnel well worth seeing. Seven shafts and about seven chains done at the north end, inverted and the brick work about done. On by engine over the East and West Junction Railway to Halford then we had to walk 3 miles in the dark to Helmdon.

The Enderby mineral branch in 1950, with an ex-Midland Johnson 3F 0-6-0 No. 43326 on an afternoon working taking coal to the quarries.

6th Jan. To engineers offices and onto Brackley viaduct which sank. The whole has been inverted and buttressed and 2 of the middle arches taken down and rebuilt. The valley is 1 part soil, 2 parts gravel, 3 parts blue clay, they hadn't founded deep enough on the blue clay and the piers started to slip together. The weight of the bank also had shoved out the gravel under the turf, the bank advanced and the turf refused to break, consequently having less space to cover it all sucked up like great worms. They hope now that all trouble is over but they are not sure. On by Route engine and an inspector nearly to Quainton road; reached about 3.30 and had nothing to eat since breakfast, the country being a desert as far as pubs are concerned.

8th Jan. Bailey and Baker have taken on the 6in side draining at 6d a yard forward which I think a good price though they wanted 7d. While I was away they ordered two engines from Hunslet and hired *Nessie* for SS. There are enquiries for setts all over the place. Leeds 5 trucks weekly. Stafford Tramways, Birmingham electric, wanting about 50,000 tons. Blackpool 2,000 ton, job got by someone else. Did not go to SS. Footner has stopped his rammel order. But Mosely wants about 500 tons a month for some months to come so we are all right. At Brackley viaduct to stop the bank from slipping. They had a concrete wall 23ft down into ground, 12ft thick at bottom and running up 12ft thick for about 20ft then off 2ft thick at top about 4ft above the ground.

11th Jan. The final (?) summing up of Lovatt's account is £7,774-2-10d for the railway and £393 for materials etc taken by us.

15th Jan. Over to SS. What is left of x heap is to go through the mills again when the rolls are new.

Nessie does junction work with Lane. *Gerald* works with Holland. *Charlie* with Burnham. *Gerald* is a better engine than *Charlie* and always has been.

19th Jan. Worked at prices till 5.45 and discovered while doing it that the wall Bromhead built for us in Bond Lane, price £61-0-6 had been added to the railway bill by Lovatts which was cheerful.

21st Jan. 5 ton crane broken, cast iron bed for bearing in the running motion underneath owing to some mud in the spur wheels pressing the bottom brass down. Tank finished riveting plates on and got into position on mill wagons. Drain sent up 8 wagons rammel settled about the agricultural drain on the Common.

25th Jan. Up to see drainers who were unloading a little rammel. To see tank on tip end. Found *Walter* off the road and rail snapped through, probably made brittle by the frost.

28th Jan. To London via Barrow 8.36, St Pancras 11.55, cab to Euston. Saw an assistant of Mr Groom, settled box to be opened, lengthened hours, trains to come before 11am to relieve traffic for rest of day.

2nd Feb. Over to Leicester and on to SS by 10.15 train with RFM. Denning (signals) Walker (traffic) and Grassman (goods). Complained we didn't give them any competitive rates, they promised to do their best for us about sidings and telephone and keep us 80 wagons in hand and trains to get traffic away and signal box hours extended 7am-8.30pm in two shifts. We may get something done now.

5th Feb. Flood rising. Over to SS, inspected wagon hurt by LNW, who have written that it was not their fault,

which it obviously was. Home 4.30. Flood still rising. Blizzard later on. Flood across road at Swithland Church.

6th Feb. Water has gone down in Swithland village. It is just not over the railway in the lowest place. Old bridge, wooden, at Loughborough lifted and had to be weighed down by wagons of rails. All traffic runs on one goods line. Much damage done to Lovatt's yard. Water running through Loughborough station like anything.

8th Feb. Big slip in bank where curve begins this side Swithland bridge, others starting.

9th Feb. Baker up without my knowing it and let Airds bridge remains to B& B for £5-10 reckoning 50 wagons at 2/3 each about. Pipes delayed through want of MR wagons, whereat B&B grumbled and rightly. Letter from Stuart saying he will want much top ballast as the line has slipped in many places owing to the floods. Great grumble from Swithland road man that he can't get his stuff carted.

19th Feb. To Yeomanry Orderly Room and into Leicester loco shed to look at roof arrangements. At SS into Lanes Hill; there was a fall there about where Bachelor was killed of about 100 tons rammel off a sloping joint, no one hit, there is a good lot of unbarring on the top.

22nd Feb. Up line 11.30 by carriage and met engineer at Swithland junction about the drain they have put in on Lord L's land[11], the man is a new one and thought, as per plan, that the land belonged to railway.

25th Feb. Found S Baum and Sexton trying to jack up a drop back into a MR wagon, it was too tight to go in properly.

2nd March. Round with GB and SPB 9.45 and valued the 2 x 10ton cranes and the 2 x 3 tons which are to be depreciated in future at 10% instead of 9½%.

11th March. Broughton has started down at Swithland junction. About snap holes – they are put in by drillers, cost 1s a foot, are drilled with #15 drills bore about 1½ inch, 3-6ft length for getting out stumps and big stones.

29th March. They are digging the pit for the new shed, entrance already done from top end. An MR wagon sheet is acting as screen in the little shed and will have to be sent away in the bottom of a wagon of broken. Saw timbers for roof being got out.

2nd April. On to SS, Lanes Hill looking much better very nearly over road there. We are not to bid more than £100 an acre for Wilsons field and shall not at present want the two Frewen plots. WB is getting about 800 tons per week from there and will get more. Two ballast trains per week knocked off by Bucks; but Cambs & Brum will take 800 each. Meanwhile to stock on the MS&L. He has a small x stock in wagons.

6th April. Chimneys and principals up on engine house roof.

22nd April. Lovatts sent down a man to say they can't take the 9in pitching at present. Baker has made them and doesn't want them valuing and messing about so he said "I am loading them and you must take what I have in the wagons" and sent wagons into quarry and loaded all that are made. He hadn't loaded any at all really. Old card!

23rd April. Fewkes said he would ask Footner to pay for siding because his ballast filled up the place, we said don't or he will take away his ballast trade. They went away in our favour. Saw Gosling, L. Lovelace's agent who promised not to be unreasonable about selling land for sidings. Pitch in at home wagons on incline to gullet got away and over the end into the railway by Cufflins Bridge. CB barely stopped men and wagons through into the quarry from colliding. It was due to the stop not being big enough.

1st May. Bill from Airds for repairs and alterations to their bridge and railway, owing to one of our engines getting approval on Sept 23rd.

18th May. Up line and cleaned out stones from upright pipes in drain. There are many keys out and the tops of many chairs chipped off. Great row re. E. Cook's crew who had not taken x away.

19th May. They have blown out a lot of the partition between the two quarries at H'cliff thinking to get for Lovatts but found to their surprise it was all good stuff. Sent out 50 Lovatts from quarry besides ballast and sand. Letter from Grassman saying you keep 800 of my wagons in stock and send out about three a day, I really can't have this. Meanwhile why should we not send Lovatt's ballast in owners and use LNW's for ordinary traffic?

20th May. Made more notes of railways. To H'cliffe. GB scared that there is not enough BV Ballast in the quarry, wants a siding down by the tip using the Airds siding points, I cordially agreed. Found Burton prying up branch, told him to count damaged chairs – result 210 going, 40 gone.

21st May. Slated Bowes about various things; he is to send Lovatt ballast in our wagons so as to give the regular traffic more to the LNW ones. Train of 50 wagons, 3 engines over 5.45!

25th May. Both sides mill working. The 2nd crane cylinder cross heads and other fittings are being got ready to replace those now in the 10 ton crane which has been very groggy for some time and won't do more than half work now. *Nessie* at SS can't get more than 30lbs steam pressure and is just about run out, not being more than £3 a week to us.

26th May. Wet, so not out till 7.30. Into gullet and watched springing of a hole. Footner has put on a ballast train again once a fortnight and Lovatt has ordered 15 wagons bottom ballast per day instead of 10, to Aylestone. Very short of work. 22 LNW wagons away at SS yesterday which will rejoice Grassman's soul.

27th May. Out 7.20. Up to 10 ton crane which is getting on slowly, on top of hill. 9am 5 ton crane broke down, one axle snapping. Also broke a stud in 3 ton crane underneath gear in an attempt to run the 5 ton out of the way. Found them riddling xx stock because so dirty, asked why not get old screen out of Quorn wood pit, said fetch next day with Buttaway.

29th May. Found Peters loading 12 Lovatts from the tips, he had loaded 60 there already without making much appreciable difference. He puts about 3 men to a wagon. Up and helped to put wheels and shaft back under 5 ton crane.

4th June. 32 wagons x out about 8 men shovelling all day, say ¾ a day, makes price about 1¼ a ton.

8TH June. Loaded out 42 wagons using guards, driver mill men etc. Walked home.

11th June. Record day for stuff sent away – total tonnage being 15,000. Finished up with a Diamond Jubilee train. 60 wagons away at about 5.40. Over to SS with RFM and GB. He has not yet started to put up incline because stone not ready. We are sending the LNW ballast away with chips etc. in it to Hawksworth Moore and another permanent way man who is only too glad to have it.

12th June. Many enquiries for tenders for 2in 4x4 and 3x6 for Saltley. Down to Swithland Junction with GB & SPB to look at slip. In loading xx from sides a man pulled up two 12ft boards and let a flood through. It took two engines to pull the wagon out and they have been shovelling underneath ever since. (11am) Home for lunch.

29th June. Three sets of boats in for x and all clamouring. The xx stock is going well, about 30 trucks. Round and saw x stock ground by wharf. To Hawcliffe with GB, loaded up 6 wagons 9in pitching for Lovatt, clearing the quarry.

2nd July. Lovatts write they can't do with more than 5 trucks rammel at present from SS. Saw Lanes Hill which is progressing well, also the incline in Cary Hill. The one engine has arrived and is working, though very stiff.

5th July. B. Butler and Saunderson met at Swithland junction 10.15 with *Willie*.

7th July. Letter from Stuart to say that he had rec'd RFM's re. complaints and repeating that we were spoiling his wagons by sprigging and that he would in future not complain but charge repairs. Lovatt had not acknowledged our way leave bill for eight months which looks like trouble. Round quarry and examined Lovatt's wagons, found about 2 sound brakes out of 19 examined.

8th July. 3,420 tons xx is the order from Barrow RDC, in this morning which is good.

12th July. At Derby saw Wittaker, coming in for end of interview RFM and RWLD being there. Result. Also saw Warrener re. MR part of SS sidings and he promised to speak to the LNW about it. Saw also Briddon's underling who asked if wagon supply was all right. Saturday Brewin at rock foot clearing place for drill, Berdinner put getters above who heaved a stone on BR's back and broke two ribs!! Cider never arrived at Stanton last Friday.

16th July. Up to top of Lanes Hill and into bottom and into Clint Hill. Bowes has been making 2in by substituting for x instead of for xx, because of being busy with xx orders. Result, beautiful 2in but mills choked and riddle choked and riddle belt breaking and about half a days break done. Ordered not to break 2in from x again but from xx. Incline into Clary Hill is done though winch not yet in.

4th Aug. Letter from GBF to say he was coming through with engineers, would I meet him at Swithland junction? Stopped and enquired on way down, old man said they were coming about 9.30, down 10.15 with *Walter*, saw Grasby who said they were coming 12.30 or thereabouts. Down 12.30 with *Willie* and sent her home, stayed till 12.45 or so and walked back. Showed Eric and Martin Tilby round mills. Saw Peters about making a crossing for Swithland end siding 1 in 5 to fit crossing chairs we have in stock.

10th Aug. 3pm collected apparatus and C. Wright and Burton and out to Swithland end where took levels and put in pegs for siding. Started 8in above ground, found the level pt on bank, took 4ft from it for c. line and drove in peg to diff, of heights so with 3 ,4 and 5, 6 finished to other side of water as far as I could level but did not do the bank.

11th Aug. Down to junction and measured distance from tank to high side, found to be 20ft. Tried with GB to tighten left crank of machine and undid back tyre to see if anything was the matter. Down 12 noon with *Willie* and guards and unloaded 18in pipes at Swithland junction, easing them down the bank with tar cord and a man in charge. The first three went owing to the cord giving but none were broken. After dinner watched repairing of 10 ton crane jib of which the end had gone. Took off pulley and iron end, cut off 4ft from jib, clinched up the timbers again and coupled things up. All done without a hitch.

12th Aug. Opened letters and down 9.45 to junction with *Willie* and high sides and loaded up the tank, getting back at 11am. Put timbers across, started with jacks, put a rope round her and the elder tree behind and eased her down with wedges on the timbers. Down in afternoon and pegged out the 1 in 20 rise for the siding, leaving 4 chains on the level.

16th Aug. Tackled wage question and found it very tough. Wrote Stuart to stop traffic Wednesday 2pm to let us put in crossing at Swithland.

30th Aug. Caledonian 10.15, started for Carlisle. Rain. Lunch at Carlisle and saw M.C. Kemp. On to Dalbeattie via Dumfries. Dalbeattie folks v. civil, called at office which is in the village beside polishing works. Newall Bros. Quarry = big face 200ft high, 2 lifts, all setts, kerbs and masonry with an antediluvian black and smooth roll and riddle with $^3/_8$ or $\frac{1}{2}$ in mesh wire for making fine gravels, fed from the squarers spoil heaps. They never fly a stone, but have two fixed cranes with 50ft of the rock face unprotected which take their chance. Saw many old MS squarers. The rock is granite softer and coarser grained than ours and the setts do not wear smooth. Tea and back to Carlisle 8.15. Slept there, much done up.

31st Aug. By 8.40 from Carlisle to Penrith and on to Threlkeld by the Reswick branch. Saw Threlkeld quarry; all work done by rope roads, narrow gauge. Drilling small compressed air drills, pressure 80lbs. They make no deeper holes than 12ft. Quarry is on 2 lifts. Squarers mostly work out of pit. Like Dalbeattie they do pretty much as they like about their powder and scouted the idea of locking the banisters. They make kerb and have a concrete slab trade and sell sand to Stuart's granolithic and are putting up sheds for a coloured tile trade, a secret they think a good one to be made with sand. They supply a lot of ballast, near 20 trucks a day to the LNW. Back to Penrith 11.48 lunch there in a pub.

7th Sept. Asked CB when I could get at the junction siding but he didn't hold out much hope for the present. Must tackle the old man. Stores requisition from Bowes for 500 sleepers, what has he done with all his Norway? We can't supply at present as we haven't the timber and Kirchen is away. Brum Wagon Company, man over to do a repair. He bagged Sturgess, Wright and Brown to work for him, labour being cheaper here as he saved the railway fares and extra time. GB told him that in future he must bring his own men and not coolly bag ours as he wants them. Telephone from WB: "MR train shunted up our branch this morning and we threatened to knock them off if they didn't shift. Junction blocked with LNW & MR loads". Round quarry and Hawcliffe with CB in afternoon.

8th Sept. Went all over quarries barring Clint Hill and saw mills and electric lighting. Tip from H Smythe (who was looking around): get $\frac{1}{4}$ lb alum to a bucket white wash and wash all over roof of engine shed to prevent sparks catching.

9th Sept. Sidings information yesterday. Midland train shunted up branch 8th 10.15, went down when threatened by WB with expulsion. Special LNW in with empties day before, not being allowed to take away fulls, was kept 4 hours shunting from down to up line unable to get into junction while we worked out traffic from the inside.

10th Sept. Junction at SS blocked with loads up to bridle path gate on our branch.

15th Sept. Into quarry and watched unsuccessful attempts by 3ton crane to pull down some heavy stones.

16th Sept. WJM and CHM over and on to SS. Round Hawcliffe and main quarry. Condemned 2 Lovatt wagons in loop line for bad brakes. A lot of the H'cliffe partition is blown out and makes much rammel with good rock behind.

17th Sept. On to Lanes Hill via Charley. The bottom is half rammel but the top looks much better and there is every appearance of a real good quarry for the future.

29th Sept. Many angry letters from the LNW especially Grassman who says that now we have transferred to the MR competition the question of extension and of broken orders will be reconsidered from a very different stand point. RFM wrote them back in suitable terms, I did most of the writing.

7th Oct. *Kathleen* in with a broken crank pin. SPB knew it was liable for some time but could not get hold of her to do any repairs which was the cause of words between him and CB. *Willie* doing

junction work in afternoon, got off road owing to facing points to old dead end not being properly closed which caused her to get on 2 roads and of course mount. The sidings men tried to make out that one of our guards was at the points at the time which was not true. Wrote letter to Warrener same evening on account.

18th Oct.
Out at 6.30 and on to Swithland Junction, found that CB had taken the gang on at 6am when old Baker told me 7am. Moreover he had pitched the top stone for the retaining wall into the slip! Worked on there barring meals till 4.30. 20 men. Used 61 wagons muck and top stone (4). They also tipped some end tips and started the loading dock.

26th Oct. A big morning for money also setts (4x5) and xx orders. Request from Amalgamated Society of Railway Servants that we should label our wagons on both sides, signed Geo Green.

1st Nov. To Sorrel 12.15. Found EM working at bridge drawings. Put my investigation on 40ft Anstey plan. Round quarry with REM after lunch, helped to unload the larch poles sent by Bowley. They are v. big and occupy 5 timber wagons (Cambrian from Three Cocks). CB shoved them round the loading dock at back of x stock ground and the strain of the curve put one of the wagons off the road.

2nd Nov. Out 7.15 Saw timber wagon pulled on rails again.

5th Nov. To Loughborough 9.2 with RFM, reached London 11.50 straight to Euston. Interviewed Harrison and Grassman together (we being three). Talked for an hour. They promise (1) to extend siding double what we asked for if we would put in our loop (2) to give us a man like Elmer to be independent of Bloxham and see to our interests in every way. Lunch about 1.15 then to Charity Commissioners & Stores and home by 4pm train.

11th Nov. Made tracing of section of SS railway showing new siding and figured up for WB.

1st Dec. RFM up and looked at sidings before lunch. *Robbie* off outside loco shed pulled on by other three. Made enquiries and found that GB has plenty of flat bottoms for new sidings (by his own account). Started to make a 40ft plan of proposed SS siding for the LNW enlarging from the 25in.

2nd Dec. Copied and forwarded letter RFM to Cloughy re Sapcote pit which the parish are talking of selling. Finished up tracing 40ft SS Railway for LNW. Round quarry and siding extension, the day men are having a high time in the quarry under G. Cheshire.

3rd Dec. At SS went over and saw Granitethorpe bed and recruited B. Church for Hobden.

8th Dec. Talk to GB over increasing rough supply and the squarers price question. Made copy of two clauses in Frewen lease, sent to Cloughy re. the proposed Top Pit aerial railway. Home from Swithland Junction.

14th Dec. At Leeds saw Prince, would he let us send some of his 3x6 to Bradford? Answer – he would want about 5,000 tons more or all our make nearly of 98 but B might have a few hundred tons if they were really in a hole. We calculated we might make by the end of year 1,000 tons more than the Leeds order if things are favourable. At Bradford, Cox asked what we could we do for him, we said 300 by March or 500 by June, a drop in the ocean, his committee were hurrying him but he would see them again and communicate meanwhile we promised to let him know before taking another big order. Price we should not raise unless we have to give our men more. Boy at MS junction is to be removed (per Smith).

31st Dec. Levelled wall end and bridge for GB. Was soaked by *Willie* bursting a tube just as she passed us and level. At SS we have bought Lanes garden but contract not yet signed so told WB to keep quiet. Lanes Hill much improved. LNW have refused to telegraph MR messages, including our wagon orders. Down and saw siding which is done except about 60 yards.

1889
19th Jan.11am talk with RFM re crane bank prices. Wrote HAR Fowler of BW Co, made proposals to make 50 or 100 new wagons at £69. 5 ton crane broke another axle.

9th March. Levelled the two bridge piers; the difference is under ¼ in. Levelled up the new siding room its rise is 1 in 66. F. over to lunch settled to keep on the present 100 hired at £9, hire 50 more at £10 for 8 years, buy 50 at £69 those to be sent to SS first to get the 1½ inch couplings parted by LNW as Clayton will only allow 1⅜ when they are once running we can bring them on here.

24th March. Letter from Griggs & Lovatt, also 25in plan of railway. Put GCR on my 6in map and on our big 25in of MS. Young Hancock over in morning, settled with him that he was to give us 2 cwt in the truck that is for 7.2 cwt consign 9 tons instead of 20½ cwt then we give up something like 2 cwt a wagon. He to pay the short weight up to now of 20 tons to give us 3d a ton off.

14th April. Staffordshire Tramways. We quoted them a price they ordered and we had to go to our lawyers to get the money out of them. Now they've ordered some more, we refused to send any. We tendered usual terms 2½ monthly or net, they wanted in a great hurry then never took any for some months. Their engineer wrote in a great stew and RWLD replied, doubtless he was not aware that we had taken proceedings to get our cash. Gave CM a lesson on railway construction all morning. Arrival of engine *Earl*.

19th April. Smith of GCR over, re. weighing machine etc; most anxious to do all we could.

22nd April. Darbishire[12] over with an engineer to look at our mill engines, lunched him. He is very anxious for us to go to Penmaenmawr both RFM and myself.

18th May. Plotted section of proposed new road as per my survey. Walters over from Brum Wagon Co. re. broken axle boxes. It is the fault of Clayton to whose specification we have to work. The spring buckles are right down on the box tops and no tops would stand that, they are ⅝ thick probably on half the MR wagons, running are smashed in the same way. Expedition with *Countess* out as far as Loughboro meadow and very successful. Letter from HEM. They are using all sorts of top ballast on the line including Groby.[13] Letter from Mackay refusing our bid for Quorn.

6th June. 1st 10 new wagons arrived via S Stanton.

8th June. Up and saw rammelling at H'cliffe again. They unload six wagons a day.

13th June. Set out a curve by RFM's method to 7'6" radius for Merritt. GB much agitated by the way boys trespass and damage the line; someone plastered an MR wagon with its own grease and filled the foxes with gravel.

14th June. To Swithland Junction with GB and Peters, settled that they should start at the bad place tomorrow and repair all through the branch.

15th June. Out to Swithland to look for any traces of Lovatt's engine they not having been down yet, heard they would probably be down in under an hour. Told Cheshire not to break the road till they were come and gone.

27th July. Leicester Master Builders & National Association of MBs over to MS about 150 of them. Gave them lunch and drinks and ran them round the quarry in a train of wagons and out to Swithland Junction where they got into their carriages again.

13th Aug. Re. Stokes; he said his colliery had had to complain to the Home Office because he never came near them and he considered he was as much responsible for Whitwick[14] as anyone (this being an adit).

26th Aug. The loco shed is at last being repaired, the wagon shop is turned out and *Willie* is to be repaired there.

30th Aug. Measured up tub roads and roads in sinking hole[15]. Saw beginning of a coat and hat place as an addition to the engine shed.

2nd Sept. Down 9.10 as had to wait and see RFM before I started, he over to Groby. GB has sold wagon iron stock to Lovatt for about 2½ times scrap price and been doing a deal for the spare wheels and axle which no doubt Lovatt will buy too.

3rd Sept. Letter from Lovatt buying our wheels for £5.10. the set whereas Mosely had written and offered £4 this is the 6 ton wheels. The Brum Wagon Co have given £7 for the 8 ton ones.

Explanatory Notes
[1] Prehistoric human bones were discovered.
[2] Rammel = loose assorted sizes of poorest quality aggregate.
[3] Midland and MR, refers to the Midland Railway Company.
[4] Henry Lovatt, contractor building the section between Leake and Aylestone of the Great Central Railway.
[5] Quoins; larger corner stones used on buildings and bridges.
[6] This indicates that in 1896 barges were still being loaded with granite on the Company's private wharf on the Grand Union Canal.
[7] John Aird & Sons, London contractors who built the Swithland Reservoir for Leicester Corporation Water Works from 1894 to 1896, via the Mountsorrel branch.
[8] Ellis. This not likely to be either John or Joseph Ellis.
[9] NH = Nunnely Hill Quarry.
[10] SS = Stoney Stanton Quarry.
[11] Lord L, Lord Lonsdale, the land owner.
[12] Darbishire, owner of the rail served Penmaenmawr Quarry on the Caernarvonshire coast, served by the LNWR.
[13] Groby Quarry, midway between Mountsorrel and Stoney Stanton Quarries to the western suburbs of Leicester; had rail connection with the Leicester & Swannington Railway, opened 13th July 1832.
[14] On 19th April 1898, a disastrous fire killed 40 men at the No.5 Pit at Whitwick Colliery, Coalville, Leicestershire.
[15] Sinking Hole = a new and deeper excavation in the quarry floor.

A dramatic line up in the early 1900s of six Hunslet 0-4-0 saddle tank locos, resplendent in their black livery and red lining, with polished brass and copper work. The two men standing on the left are shunters, armed with their traditional hooked poles for working chain couplings. Lafarge Aggregates.

THE BARON

3. MOUNTSORREL QUARRY
And Barrow-on-Soar Rail Loading out Terminal

Mountsorrel granite has been used locally for centuries as a building stone, with its chippings used for the highway. Quarrying on a commercial scale was carried out as early as 1812, when a Mr Jackson took a lease from the Earl of Lanesborough for a small quarry on the fringe of Buddon Wood. From the Earl's modest workings, Mr Jackson had extended his activities to employ a hundred men over the next decades. In 1842 the lease was sold to Mr John Martin, who continued to work Buddon Wood quarry until 1848, when he took over the entire mineral extraction lease, including the Mountsorrel area. In 1854, the Mountsorrel Granite Company was formed and adopted a windmill as its trade mark, based on the mill that surmounted Broad Hill. During 1869-70, this area became the main quarry; it was extended into Broad Hill and the windmill had to be demolished.

The granite industry expanded with the growth of civic Britain, and local councils' need for road setts and kerb stones. Of course, this could only happen once the transport of these weighty products to a much wider market became possible. The Leicester Navigation canal had opened as early as 1794, from Loughborough south to Leicester, and two weeks later the Grand Union Canal opened to London, terminating at the Great Wharf, Paddington. The Mountsorrel Granite Co soon took advantage of the canal on its doorstep, providing a wharf quay and dry dock for barge repairs. The Canal Committee actively sought out the stone traffic which produced a good steady business, going both north and south. Unexpectedly, the canal company had been receiving poor returns from coal – lower than had been anticipated from the Derbyshire collieries.

Mountsorrel's granite traffic increased considerably to the north where many towns were rapidly expanding during the Industrial Revolution. New manufacturing meant more people and houses for them, and paved roads. In the period 1779 to 1841, the canal company paid very high dividends, but these were soon reduced on the opening of the Leicester & Swannington Railway.

An Act of Parliament for a branch line from the Midland Counties Railway 'to the Town of Mountsorrel in the County of Leicester' was passed as early as March 1837, in the first year of the Reign of Queen Victoria. Nothing came of this and a further Act followed in August 1859. It was declared that: *whereas the said Railway Company (now the Midland Railway Co) have not made the said Branch Railway authorised, whereby the Inhabitants of the said Town and the neighbourhood thereof, and the Proprietors of certain valuable Quarries of Granite and other Materials there, and the Public generally, have been deprived of the Benefits intended to be conferred by the said Act.*

The engineer for this Mountsorrel Railway was John Addison and the details of the survey had been deposited in the office of the Clerk of the Peace for the County of Leicester the year before, on 30 November 1858 'at 12 o'clock at noon, signed by Mr Freer,

A blasting at Mountsorrel in May 2008; these took place at around 12.30 each day, with thousands of tons brought down each time. The previous working 'benches' (they had a lovely pink glow to them) are clear to see.

Clerk' The undertaking would be called the Mountsorrel Railway, *and built with all proper conveniences and works. The Branch line will connect with the main line, 3,360 yards to the north of the mile and gradient post, being 21½ miles from Derby and 29 miles from Rugby, in the Parish of Barrow-on-Soar, and terminating near to the quarry bridge (north end) in the town of Mountsorrel. The Railway shall be completed within four years of the passing of the Act. A deposit (Bond) in the sum of £664, being 8% of the amount of the estimate of the expenses of erecting signals, works and conveniences and the wages of such watchmen, switchmen, etc; shall be repaid by the proprietors of The Railway to the Midland Railway Co at the end of every half year.*

The main sponsor of the new railway was the Fifth Earl of Lanesborough, John George Danvers Butler, of Swithland Hall. A clause stipulated that: *The Earl of Lanesborough or his heirs shall, on opening the said Railway for the public conveyance of passengers, give such proof to the satisfaction of the Lords of the said*

Left. **The westerly Bond Lane over bridge in 1910, with the rails heading towards the Hawcliff Quarry. This is likely to be one of the bridges set-out and supervised by the young W.F.Martin. Ian Brown.**

Below. **A gathering of nearly 100 men and one dog in a portrait dating from the 1890s; white beards on the senior men and the universal protective head-gear of the period, the cloth cap. Ian Brown.**

Top. Construction of the Mountsorrel Railway western branch to Swithland Sidings in1892. At top left a horse drawn cart takes away some of the overburden of soil (some way to go!) while below two steam vertical boilers provide power for drills. Ian Brown.

Middle. Six plank open wagons owned by the quarry company, loading up with asphalt sold under the trade name of 'Targranite' in June 1921. Wagon No.559 has the two blue oval enamel signs with details as to ownership and return destination.

Bottom. The beautifully turned out No.31 THE COUNTESS, at Mountsorrel where she was delivered new in 1898; this loco also worked for a while at the Enderby Quarry. Frank Jones.

committee. Whether it was ever envisaged that passenger trains would run on the line or whether this was a way of getting the Bill through Parliament we cannot know but the passenger provisions were never pursued. After all, the quarry ensured its almost continuous operation and there were few locals to use it.

The junction with the Midland Railway at Barrow-on-Soar was on the level and immediately began a short stretch at 1 in 61 down, to cross the Soar valley on the level for 48 chains, then on a gradient up of 1 in 67 for 36 chains to cross the river navigation by a soaring single brick arch of 85ft span at a height of 40ft above water level. The track then levelled out over the main street in Mountsorrel on another brick bridge, 16ft high with a span of 40ft. This was replaced in 1898 by a single span girder bridge built by the Leicester firm of W. Richards & Son, who are still a major engineering company to this day. The later western extension of the railway to Swithland Sidings on the Great Central Railway was carried out under the terms of the original Act.

The magnificent brick bridge still spans the old navigation, now happily used by pleasure boaters. The date of 1860 is prominent on both sides of the single span arch, picked out in contrasting bricks. This was by a long way the major engineering work. The long embankment, equally impressive in its way, was, in commendably economic fashion, made up of spoil from the quarry itself. A large stone tipping dock was built alongside the river bridge, immediately on the quarry (west) side of the navigation, served by a siding from the quarry. Immediately the quarry tracks passed over the road bridge a single siding to the south side descended steeply down to water level, by a 'switch-back'; internal dumb buffered wood wagons were taken down and loaded directly into barges. Alongside the siding was a dry dock with timber stanchions built over it, to permit barges to be lifted out for repairs. At

some time in the 1920s, the switch-back track was modified with a single track on a steep gradient to the canal wharf.

The mineral branch made a gentle curve to the north at Barrow-on-Soar to connect with the MR main. A long siding had a short loop to the south and there were a series of crossover points in both directions. There were five sidings, spanning a tunnel which permitted a single standard gauge track to pass underneath, connecting to limestone pits and workings to the north-east side of the MR. There were over twenty limestone kilns on the west side, adjacent to the granite company's works. By 1903 the exchange sidings had been increased, and at the triangle formed by the lime works railway tracks a large concrete manufacturing plant had been set up to replace the lime works.

In 1923 Captain C.H. Martin, whose grandfather had acquired the original Quorn Wood quarry in 1842, was the managing director. Six years later quarrying was taking place into the main hill. Further isolated quarries for stone extraction were made at Cocklow Wood Quarry, No.4 Quarry and Hawcliffe Quarry. The colours of the hornblende granite varied from a warm rose colour to subtle shades of green/blue. Hawcliffe quarry, to the west of the main quarry operations, was being developed at the turn of the last century, with two distinct

rail branches connecting to the works with a long spoil tip line. By this time the westerly branch to Swithland sidings on the Great Central had been made, and the Hawcliffe site had been made into a concrete making plant served by a siding. By the 1920s this had been converted into a road tar surfacing plant.

The line to the GC had originally been little more than a siding for the supply of material, earth fill and so on for the construction of the Great Central Railway to the west. It had been made by Henry Lovatt, who had the contract to build the section between East Leake and Aylestone, some 16½ miles, between the years 1893 to 1898. The line had been upgraded at intervals for stone traffic to the GCR. From the rail over bridge at Mountsorrel to the exchange sidings at Swithland, close by the reservoir of that name, was 1½ miles. The final curve southward into the Swithland sidings was of 13 chains, mostly on a downward gradient. On the inner section of this curve were two sidings, one a short spur of 60 yards, and the other terminating just before the triple road bridges, a couple of hundred yards long. Swithland had five sidings, four of which were loops. Midway there was a signal box with a clear view of all the tracks, and this remains in place to this day. Along the mineral branch was the small Nunkley Hill Quarry, nearly half a mile from the junction. This quarry lay beside

One of the few Pecketts DORIS, delivered new in 1928, with her proud driver Mr Wakeling. This loco also served part of her time at Enderby Quarry and is seen here around 1950. Frank Jones.

Top. Hunslet No.17 VIOLET of 1913. Most of her life was spent at Mountsorrel but in November 1934 she was transferred to Stoney Stanton quarries. Frank Jones.

Middle. 'PIXY', an early Hunslet of 1874, sold out of service in 1891 to the contractor T. Oliver. Frank Jones, courtesy David W. Webb.

Below. Manning Wardle 0-4-0ST FAIRY of 1862, which worked alongside 'PIXY'. It had been purchased from contractor T. Rennie & Co when one year old, and then sold on in 1896 to Holme & King. Collection David W. Webb.

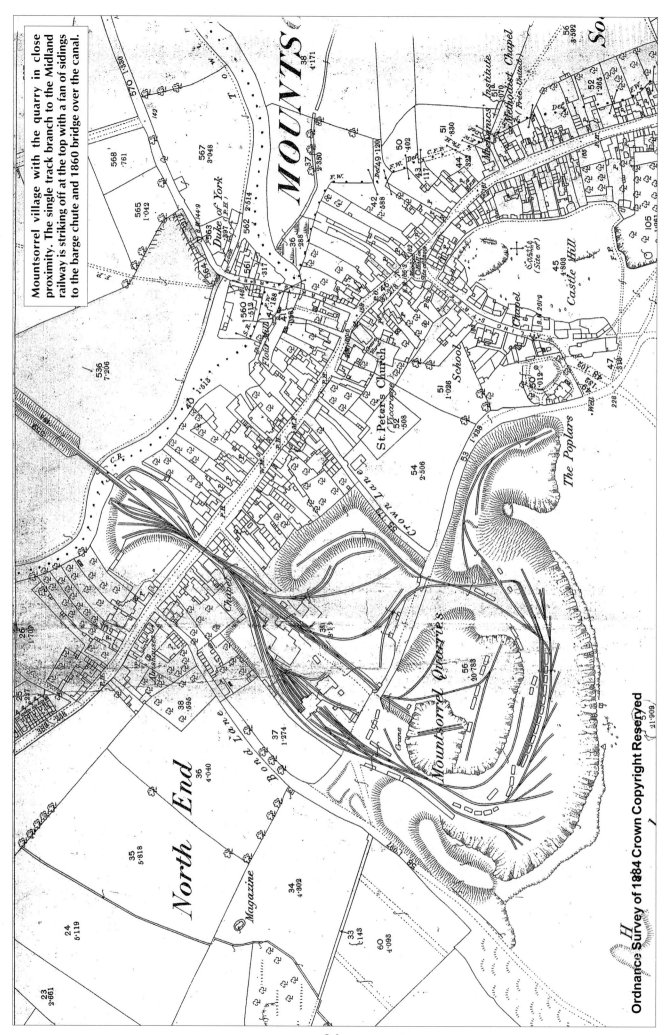

Mountsorrel village with the quarry in close proximity. The single track branch to the Midland railway is striking off at the top with a fan of sidings to the barge chute and 1860 bridge over the canal.

North End

St. Peter's Church

MOUNTS

Castle Hill

The Poplars

Mountsorrel Quarries

Ordnance Survey of 1884 Crown Copyright Reserved

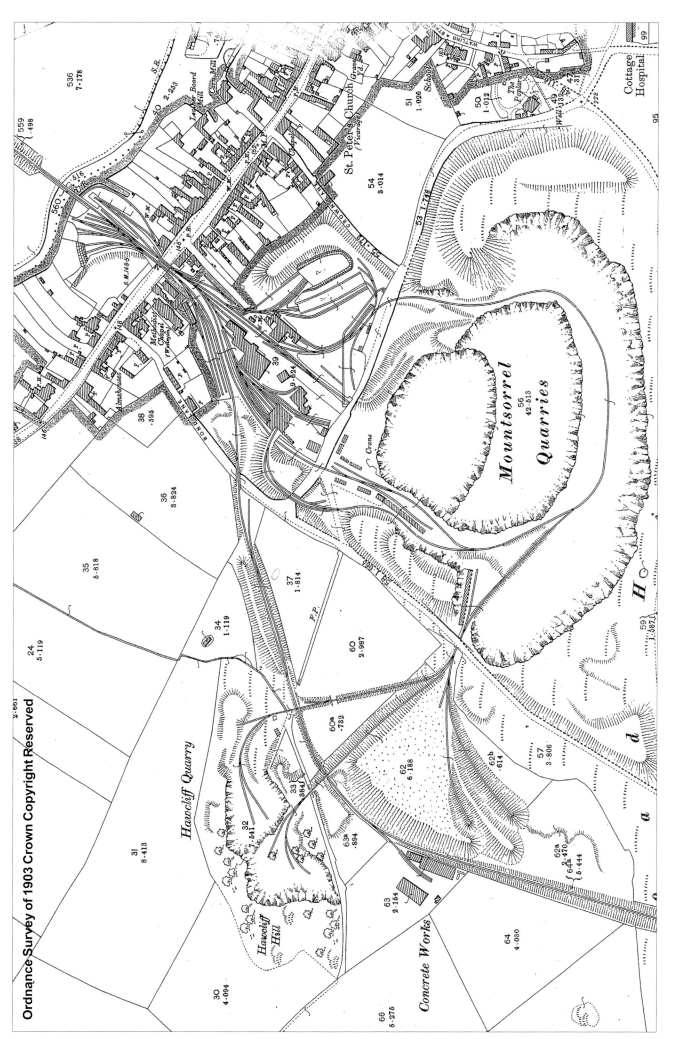

Ordnance Survey of 1903 Crown Copyright Reserved

Mountsorrel Quarries

Hawcliff Quarry

Hawcliff Hill

Concrete Works

St. Peter's Church

Cottage Hospital

25

THE BARON and crew pose for their picture during a break in shunting. Built in 1899 by Hunslet (works No.702) this 0-4-0ST lasted some sixty years until scrapped in 1959. The headlamp in front of the chimney is an unusual feature, suggesting night work was required, or at least late afternoon work in winter. Frank Jones.

Delivered new in 1900, LADY WINIFRED was finally scrapped in October 1958. The bullhead rails with wooden 'keys' and short lengths of rail are typical quarry 'make do's'. Frank Jones.

Internal quarry wagons with canvas/leather protective flaps to keep axle boxes free of dust. On the right are heaps of prepared stone setts for road making. Lafarge Aggregates.

the Rothley Plain road over bridge, and had two sidings off a loop, with a further three sidings a short distance to the west. This section of the mineral line ran in the Nunkley Hill in a cutting, so exposing the rock for quarrying. As noted in the diaries of W.F. Martin, this bridge was set out by him on 6th June 1896.

The early Mountsorrel quarry was bounded to the south-east by Crown Lane, and to the north-east by Bond Lane. To the south a lane connected these two roads, railway tracks crossing it on the level at three points. To the south of this dividing lane was the main quarry which had a circular track connecting with numerous spur branches into the main working faces. Alongside this circular track were some 26 sheds for the 'squarers' making their granite road setts and kerb stones. To the south a series of shifting tracks fed the ever changing spoil tips. By 1900 the main works were extensive; there were engine sheds for the modest stud

of locomotives, wagon repair shops and engineers shops.

Cocklow Wood Quarry, west of Hawcliff Quarry and later known as Buddon Wood Quarry opened in 1906 but was closed during the last war. It was brought back into working, rail-served, in the 1960s.

Three locomotives were in use from an early date. Chaplin built two vertical boilered 0-4-0Ts in 1860 and 1861 and these were working from 1872 and 1866 respectively. Another 0-4-0T came from

Private loading dock served by a rail siding where side tipping wagons had to be used. The barge has planks so that the road setts can be distributed evenly by wheel barrow, an important job for the bargee. Lafarge Aggregates.

The Mountsorrel crushing plant with its seven sidings (see plan page 25). The elegant gas lamp stands close by to a Hunslet saddle tank loco, with its extra large dumb buffers. Lafarge Aggregates.

The far end of the crushing plant in 1923, with the usual confusion of bits and pieces including split spoke wheel sets and piles of new timber rail sleepers. Lafarge Aggregates.

Fletcher Jennings in 1865. A Manning Wardle of 1862 was acquired from a contractor a year after it was built, and these were to be followed by a succession of eleven new 0-4-0STs from the Hunslet Engine Co Ltd, delivered over the period 1874-1920; the last new steam loco to arrive at Mountsorrel was a Peckett, in 1928. Over the years frequent locomotive transfers took place between the several Leicestershire quarries within the company. Most of the steam locos were given personal names associated with the directors, their wives or the local gentry.

The last new loco, the Peckett mentioned above, was of particular interest in that it warranted a personal letter from the builders to the senior engine driver, Mr George Wakeling. George was typical of many families who worked for one firm all their lives and he spent the best part of fifty years with the Mountsorrel Granite Quarry

Top. View from the main quarry in 1910 looking east to the high level discharge sidings. In the centre are three vertical boilers mounted on rails, and further to the right are vast piles of road setts; beyond, the embankment of the mineral line to the Midland Railway can just be seen. Lafarge Aggregates.

Middle and bottom. Mountsorrel village with quarry in the background in 1910, looking south-west over the bridge spanning the Soar Navigation. The enlargement shows the company's canal dry dock, with barges being loaded from side tipping wagons. Lafarge Aggregates.

Company. It is a testimony to his respected position that Pecketts, in a letter of 23rd January 1928, said that they 'hoped that the new locomotive will give every satisfaction', and that they had sent a framed bromide photograph of the locomotive 'per L.M.S. Railway passenger train, carriage paid'. The Wakeling family gave excellent service to the company; great grandfather George the engine driver, and father Stanley a time-served carpenter, joiner and engineer, each worked for the quarry firm their entire lives.

Carpenters and smiths shops provided for daily repairs and maintenance to the locomotives and the numerous wagons. The internal user wooden dumb buffered wagons were built in the carpenters shop, using wheelsets from the Birmingham Wagon Co; the smiths fashioned the remainder of the steel work. These home-made wagons were gradually replaced in the 1920s by steel tipping wagons, more suitable for loading by mechanical shovels. They were more in evidence after the 1930s, when granite sett and kerb stone production ceased, as they were replaced by concrete kerbs and tarmac road surfacing across the country. The making and use of setts and kerb stones in fact had all but finished by 1936. Among the work of the smiths was the routine sharpening of the star shaped drill bits. A five ton overhead crane was available in the workshops as were sheer legs outside in the yard, for lifting wagons and locomotives to remove wheels. The Mountsorrel Granite Co Ltd charged a

Top. The Mountsorrel crushing plant in 1910 with its covered loading for wagons. The private wagons are interesting, in three differing styles. Lafarge Aggregates.

Middle. One of several sidings in the 1890s which served the stone setters and their sheds; in the distance one of the Hunslet locos is approaching with wagons which will be loaded up by hand with the road setts. Lafarge Aggregates.

Bottom. In the quarry at the working faces, with dumb buffer wagons being laboriously loaded in 1880. Lafarge Aggregates.

demurrage of 3/- per day from their customers for all their private main line wagons detained beyond 48 hours, so as to ensure a quick turn-round. Without this incentive, many customers were in the habit of using wagons as a convenient means of storage.

During the 1870s between 500 and 600 men and a few boys were employed. Blasting was carried out most days, with rope netting and lengths of heavy chain laid over the quarry face to minimise flying blocks. Larger boulders were 'shotted' with extra charges of two to three ounces of powder. The rock was selected for either setts and squared slabs for paving, with broken stone or chips used for road surfacing. The smaller rocks were wheeled in barrows to the squarers sheds, in their rows. Boys would work under the guidance of fathers and other family members. Men were paid on measured estimates as piece work, but there were many abuses, such as building the squarred stone stockpiles with hollow centres! The employers soon caught on to this dodge and so weighing machines were brought into use.

Many varieties of hammer were used, the heaviest at 28lb and called a 'big buster', square and obtusely pointed at the other end. Even the 'little buster' was a still-hefty 2lb. There were others; the 'little chopper', 'big chopper', 'nobbing hammer', 'big hammer', 'big sledge and little sledge', 'peck & hack' and the small 'squaring hammer'.

In the crushing plant there were two Blakes stone crushers which produced 120 tons a day. Toothed rollers, cheaper to use, dealt with poorer quality stone. Drilling was later carried out by using steam from portable boilers on rail tracks which were constantly moved around the working areas. In turn, pneumatic drills with an Ingersol portable air compressor came into use; today lasers are used with diamond tipped drill bits. In 1923 a new screening plant was installed, with two 40ft chain hung rotary screens; the stone passed through a smooth roller mill and then a

Top. **Hawcliffe Quarry in its earlier stages of granite extraction in 1923. Rail sidings seem to run around almost everywhere, with a loco in the centre and wagons discharging spoil. Lafarge Aggregates.**

Middle. **An abandoned working brought back to life in the 1950s. A deeper pit is served by a rail incline which takes wagons to the crane in the middle distance. Lafarge Aggregates.**

Bottom. **The vast main quarry about 1900 with three working faces. In the middle distance a loco is shunting; in the centre is one of the road stone setters sheds and the familiar accompanying piles of prepared road setts. Lafarge Aggregates.**

Mountsorrell Quarry in 1910 with some dumb buffer, wooden wagons at the foot of the twin tracked incline. A second and newer conveyor belt is brining spoil up from a lower level pit.

fine mesh to give the required particle size. Stone 'elevators', driven by two Brush induction motors, discharged into 800 tons capacity hoppers above the rail tracks, each wagon being weighed once full.

For local deliveries there were two Sentinel steam road wagons and one Foster steam tractor with a trailer. Fine aggregate was supplied in the 1930s to John Ellis & Sons at their concrete product works at Barrow-on-Soar on the former lime kilns site. Here were made

paving slabs, tubes and architectural stone products, such as roof beams, stairs and flooring. There were fence posts and even railway signal posts, too. The John Ellis & Sons offices still stand today, the company name emblazoned over the entrance doorway of the 1930s building opposite the road entrance to the site. The tarmacadam plant at Hawcliffe Quarry was supplied by Messrs Gimson & Co Ltd; of Leicester in 1923, with elevators and conveyors of bucket type by Messrs Fraser &

Chalmers Engineering Works, Erith, which produced 60/70 tons per hour of Hornblende stone.

By the 1920s Barrow-on-Soar had some thirty lime kilns, and had been producing lime and plaster since 1888. John Ellis & Sons were merged with the Mountsorrel Granite Co in January 1920 and continued trading under their original name. The site alongside the MR (soon to be LMS) line occupied fifty acres on both sides of the railway, connected by the under pass single track which then fanned out to many sidings in the stock yards. John Ellis & Sons also had lime works at Kilby Bridge, about 1½ miles south of Wigston Magna station on the LMS line. A Private Siding Agreement was made on 27th May 1924 for a siding to the north which included a tipping dock to serve the 3ft gauge internal railway system. Two 0-4-0 saddle tank locomotives worked here until it closed in 1931. At the firm's Kilby South Pits, the company entered into another agreement, dated 5th July 1873, for several sidings to the south of the Midland line. These sidings were shunted by a Hunslet 0-4-0ST named WALTON, works number 458, which was later sent to the Barrow works, whereupon Manning Wardle 0-6-0ST No.1440 FRANK of 1899 arrived. This loco was in turn despatched, in November 1899, to C. Baker & Son at Wigston Station. FRANK was of class K, the most numerous of some 250 locomotives built during the period 1864-1914.

Piles of prepared setts around the setters sheds in 1910. A sheer-legs crane lifts stone up from a deeper pit; in the foreground wagons are loaded with some heavy plant for the crushing machines. Lafarge Aggregates.

Hunslet 0-4-0ST of 1899 THE BARON. In the right background is the large engine shed (note the smoke vents) with the engineering workshops next door. Both GCR, MR and Mountsorrel wagons are in evidence. There is a water colour 'interpretation' of this scene on page 70. Lafarge Aggregates.

John Ellis & Sons had some seventy 5 ton 8 cwt six-plank wagons with central drop-down doors to both sides, capacity about 13 tons. The livery was a light grey with black solebars and ironwork, and white small letters reading: JOHN ELLIS & SONS LTD; BARROW LIME WORKS, LEICESTER, with the tare and wagon number also in white. With the transfer of business to Potters Marston in 1937, these wagons found their way into the common 'pool' system during the last war.

John Ellis with his brother Joseph as a partner had a corn and malt business operating from their farm from 1827. John Ellis was involved with the Leicester & Swannington Railway from 1832 and sold coal from the West Bridge Wharf in Leicester. He also sold lime and so he rented land at Barrow from 1840; during the following forty years the business expanded dramatically. The company also traded in slates from both Groby and Swithland Quarries. With burgeoning railway development, the Ellis company built depots for its goods from the 1850s up to 1969, in which time there had been a total of 97 depots. These ranged through Leicestershire across several counties to Middlesex. John Ellis lived at Beaumont Leys, and as a director of the Leicester & Swannington supervised certain aspects of its construction when it was found that the contractor had used sub-standard lime mortar in culverts and other structures.

The line to Barrow-on-Soar from Mountsorrel quarry was finally lifted in 1979 and replaced by a conveyor belt system, which required protective cladding over bridges. New plant at the quarry included a primary crusher, one of only seven of its type in the country; it is a 'pestle and mortar' type which receives rough stone, up to a tonne or more, from 100 tonne capacity dump trucks. These are loaded at the working areas by 280 tonne excavators. Conveyors take the initial crushed stone to a pile (capacity 140,000 tonnes) for screening to size.

The stone is taken through three further crushing stages and then to twelve giant vibratory screens. Various sizes are collected into bins, each with its own conveyor, for Readymix concrete, drystone products and asphalt - in the latter case two plants coat the stone with bitumen. The rail ballast stone is treated to reduce dust and weighed at the works before transfer to Barrow via the one mile conveyor belt. At Barrow there are eight storage bins which hold 1,500 tonnes making them capable of loading one train, while a second train can be loaded direct from the quarry conveyor. Four additional bins hold 700 tonnes of 14mm, 10mm,

Looking west in 1920 with the workshops in the centre and engine shed to the left; on the right are the numerous sidings serving the crushing plant and wagon 'loading out'. Lafarge Aggregates.

An early scene of about 1876; steam is being provided from a vertical boiler to work a timber crane. Setters small sheds in the middle and signs of recent track lifting, c.1911.

A rail mounted compressor built in the Company's workshops, utilising a former dumb buffered rail wagon chassis. The newness of its construction in 1920 probably justified this photograph. Lafarge Aggregates.

Right. Rail-mounted steam boiler c1890 and built by Abbott & Co Ltd of Newark, for providing steam to drills at the working faces. This is near the workshops, with the wagon lift sheer-legs in the background. Lafarge Aggregates.

Below. Ruston and Proctor steam shovel with a home-made corrugated iron sheet cladding protection in 1913, which may have been tried at Mountsorrel Quarry.

Top. A sett maker at his craft in the 1900s. Within the next thirty years this once vast trade would be a thing of the past. The few setts that are required now are fashioned by machines. Lafarge Aggregates.

Middle. Mechanical shovel loading 'fine stone' in the quarry, into the new metal side tipping rail wagons in the late 1920s. These had a greater capacity than the traditional timber dumb buffered type. Progress was on its way. Lafarge Aggregates.

Bottom. The western branch of the Mountsorrel Railway to Swithland junction and sidings under construction in1892. In the foreground, what looks like an under bridge is being built with local stone. Lafarge Aggregates.

6mm and dust. Drilling is carried out each day using two pneumatic drills which make 110mm holes to a depth of 18 meters. These are detonated each weekday at 12.30pm. The blasting produces between 25,000 and 30,000 tonnes of rock in a wide variety of sizes. Over 50% of Lafarge's granite production at Mountsorrel is sent out by rail, around 2,500,000 tonnes in a year. The quarry occupies around 450 acres and has 100 employees. The French parent company was established in 1833 and employs 75,000 people in 75 countries.

Besides supplying Network Rail with rail ballast over a wide area, stockpiles are maintained at Lafarge/Network Rail depots at Doncaster and Toton, and at Crewe and Whitemoor. By 2009, 'PGA' two axle hopper wagons were used, as well as two train formations made up of the self-discharge wagons and conveyor wagon. The following list indicates the rail stone terminals and how they were served:- *(opposite)*

Another stone terminal had been opened at Boston Harbour, Lincolnshire, in 2002 with an investment of £887,500, but this is currently 'mothballed' and thus

'PGA' two axle bottom unloading hopper wagons	'SDT' self-discharge wagon train sets
Radlett, Herts	*Chelmsford, Essex*
Norwich Trowse, Norfolk	*Stevenage*
Elstow, Beds; also SDT	*Peterborough*
Barham/Kennet, Suffolk	*Cambridge*
Broxbourne, Herts; also SDT	*Northampton*
	Luton
	Wellingborough

not in use. During the spring of 2009 there were daily trains of 1,750 tonnes to Westbury in Somerset, linking up with the stone trains from both Hanson Aggregates and the former Foster Yeoman quarries (now Aggregates Industries). These trains consist of PGA wagons, usually around twenty five in number. A special 20mm, double screened and washed ballast has been supplied to Network Rail for its 'Stoneblower' machines. These are a new innovation compared to the more traditional tamping machines. The Stoneblower lifts each sleeper and pneumatically injects ballast into the void without disturbing the base coat of ballast. This procedure has been in use since 2007, supplying 1.1 million tonnes

of rail ballast each year in SDT and bogie box wagons to Network Rail. Redland Aggregates first stone terminal was at Radlett which opened in August 1978. The location was an old sand and gravel pit dating from the 1940s, so the ground formations are undulating, requiring a cutting and an embankment to enable bottom discharge from PGA wagons. There are six concrete supply bunkers which hold 400-500 tonnes; with the stock yard there is a total capacity of 16,000 tonnes. There are further four bunkers fed directly by a JCB.

In 1969 an asphalt coating plant was installed. To keep the merry-go-round train moving over the bottom discharge hoppers, and because there is a restricted sight line for the locomotive drivers, Redland engineers designed and made a signalling system, approved by British Rail, which aided the driver in positioning wagons over the point of discharge. As part of Redland

The heart of the quarry with one of the several vertical boilers and its attendant water tank and coal wagon; drilling is taking place and dust flying up into the air, prior to a blasting. Lafarge Aggregates.

Aggregates forward looking policy of rail usage, forty PGA two-axle hopper wagons were ordered from Standard Wagon Co Ltd of Redditch, in 1978. These were 22ft 3ins long with central solebar-mounted hopper controls, with a short handbrake and Gloucester floating axle suspension. They had decking at high level to each end with ladder access at both ends. They were painted in a pale aqua green with 'Redland' in bold large red letters of upper and lower case. They were still in use as late as 1995.

In 1989 Redland made a unique innovation in stone distribution, with the introduction of two train sets of hopper wagons with self discharge. This involved a continuous conveyor belt beneath each wagon which carried the stone to a special discharging wagon at one end. This has a conveyor jib which is slewed out to either side and delivers the stone to where it is required at the track side or at a depot. Later PHA wagons ('P' indicates two axles, 'PH' is the TOPS code, 'A' indicates air-brakes) were equipped with a Lister Petter HL 4008 diesel engine, to power the conveyor belt. Capacity of these wagons is averaged at 36 tonnes. Two unloading jibbed wagons to permit lineside discharge were built in 1985 by Standard Wagon; they measure 67ft 4ins in length, and run on Sambre et Meuse VNH1 bogies. Livery is a light shade of green with grey solebars and running gear. The lettering was bold upper and lower case 'Redland' on a red background and smaller serif letters below reading 'Aggregates' on a grey background. Early in 2009 the Lafarge fleet of PGA wagons were purchased by DB Schenker of Germany, with the few remaining Redland liveried wagons being withdrawn. On a visit in May 2008 I noted several ex-RMC red-liveried type PHA bogie hopper wagons, built in 1986 by Standard Wagon with the

Top. Work on a cutting during construction of the western branch to the GCR about 1895. The temporary track on the left is occupied by a boiler providing steam to the drills and a crane hauling rocks. Lafarge Aggregates.

Middle. Drilling the rock face in preparation for blasting. The drill requires steel rod braces and jacks to maintain the tension; the bucket of water is to keep the bits cool whilst drilling into the hardest of stone. Lafarge Aggregates.

Bottom. At the working face of the quarry with a boiler serving up steam for the rail mounted crane. All three views were taken in 1923. Lafarge Aggregates.

'RMC lozenge' and 'Roadstone' painted out, in one of the three storage sidings at Barrow, It would appear that these were never put into Lafarge use as they were sold on by the end of the year. The total number of SDT wagons is 160.

The track layout at Barrow-on-Soar was remodelled in 1978 with the aid of a Section 8 Grant when the branch line to the quarry was closed. The grant enabled the ageing BR 'HTV' two axle steel wagons to be replaced by 38 tonne PGA wagons (51 tonne glw – gross laden weight) payload wagons built by Standard Wagon of Heywood, and the opening of seven rail terminals. The fleet of PGA wagons numbered 111 in 1982, all painted in the pale green with large red letters of Redland. There were two sets of 42 wagons with four spare on planned maintenance, and another set of 23 ex-Tilbury Roadstone PGAs, numbered TBR 14500-14522. In 1987 the two 42 wagon sets, carrying 1,575 tonnes per train, 2,142 glw, transported one million tonnes to Radlett depot. Redland Aggregates hired a fleet of 51 tonne glw POA (two axle, air braked) grab discharge box wagons from Standard Wagon through the firm Railease; the payload was the same as a PGA of 38 tonnes. Coalville firm Marcroft Engineering rebuilt these wagons from former 'PEA' tip-air bulk powder wagons. The barrels were removed and a new body built on strengthened frames. These were painted dark grey in 1987, and were used for three new terminals, at Banbury for the M40 construction, Cambridge and Langley Junction near Stevenage.

The Barrow-on-Soar rail 'loading out' terminal ('loading out' is a term for any place where conveyor belts discharge into wagons) now has two reception sidings parallel to the main line. Access to the exchange sidings is controlled by Leicester power box, with all the points on private property switched by hand. From the reception sidings a diamond

Top. **Inside the Mountsorrel power house in 1923; the machinery was always kept in immaculate condition. The 'Robey of Lincoln' generator seen here did not let its operator down. Lafarge Aggregates.**

Middle. **The large flywheel and ball regulator, maintained in perfect condition. The fine coach lining applied to most surfaces, all hand polished, indicates the pride taken in the place. Lafarge Aggregates.**

Bottom. **The turbines producing electricity, with the control panels on the left; travelling overhead crane to service the plant. Lafarge Aggregates.**

crossover is used to marshal trains and empty wagons into three storage sidings at the south end. There are two wagon loading sidings which pass under the loader, overlooked by the cabin controller who also operates the loading chutes to the wagons from the conveyor above. On the south east side a single cripple siding runs under a covered area with wagon repairs carried out by Wabtec; this siding also has an adjacent yard for storage of wheel sets and so on. The controller has two screens which indicate the volumes of stone and weight of each wagon as it is loaded. He controls the loading chute with one handle, and with the other he is in full control of the Lafarge remote controlled shunting locomotive. It is a long way indeed from the days of saddle tanks WALTON and FRANK!

When an empty train arrives at the reception siding, it permits the now previously loaded train to pull forward into the north yard. The remote loco, which has pushed the entire train of wagons under the loading chute, then backs down across the diamond crossover points, to be followed by the newly arrived empty train. The shunting loco is then controlled from the rail supervisors cabin and very slowly pushes the wagons and its hauling locomotive, usually a class 66, under the loading chute once again. To the north side of the twin loading tracks there are several sidings which include a fairly recent short locomotive spur with an open ended shed for visiting locomotives to refuel. There is a bogie ballast wagon, converted with built-up staging, to enable engineers to carry out repairs to the wagon loading chutes. In a normal weekday this plant dispatches 5½ thousand tonnes of aggregate every day, with the daily PGA trains of 23 wagons carrying 1,750 tonnes per trip. Recently, for their Crewe and Doncaster traffic, Network Rail have brought into use new IOA (E) bogie box wagons with

Top. **This formidable machinery, seen here in 1923, was the stone crusher, in the yard by the workshops – toothed rollers with their drive gearing and a fly wheel. Behind are stacks of new timber sleepers, awaiting the platelayers. Lafarge Aggregates.**

Middle. **EWS class 66 diesel No.66018 hauls a train of thirty-five PGA wagons in May 2004 which have discharged their aggregate at the Elstow Stone Terminal. The main line runs alongside the depot's twin loop sidings, hidden behind the trees. Ian Brown.**

Bottom. **The Elstow Stone Terminal, a mile south of Bedford in 2004, with its radial distributor which stacks up to ten grades of stone. The train of Lafarge Aggregate PGA wagons are being hauled into the private sidings behind a class 66 loco. Ian Brown.**

Above. Trowse Stone Terminal at Norwich and its own shunter, a four wheel diesel hydraulic rebuilt by Thomas Hill Ltd in 1967 from a Sentinel, No.9401 dating back to 1950. Ian Brown.

Below. The Lafarge Chelmsford Stone Terminal looking east from the base of the steep incline up to the main line near the passenger station in September 2000. The buildings in the distance mark the former Royal Mail unloading depot.

extended top raves, built in Poland by Swidnica Przedmiescie and delivered new via Aachen and Hamburg.

Redland and now Lafarge have been responsible for a number of very forward-looking innovations, the self discharge train being one. At the Barrow loading area probably the most radical departure from traditional practice has been the use of remote controlled locomotives, as described above. Prior to their introduction however, another unusual system was in use, from August 1978 to at least August 1983; 'Roltug' cable haulage. The arrangements comprised an endless steel rope between a power winch and drum with a take-up wheel underground at the other end of the siding. This was installed on loading siding No.1, nearest to the elevated control cabin. The drive winch was located near to the present diesel loco shed to the north end of the sidings, with the take-up winch to the southern end of the wagon maintenance workshops. The wire cable was attached to both ends of a heavy steel 'mule' which ran on narrow gauge rails set between the standard gauge track. The rope was kept within the track confines by a series of 'jockey' wheels. The mule bogie had 'arms' which pressed against the wheels of the wagons above it. The operator in his cabin then moved the train under the loader, as required. On arrival of an empty train, the first wagon was shunted over the mule, and by moving the winch rope, so the arms expanded and engaged onto the wagon wheels. Once engaged and locked into position, the operator in the control

cabin would then start the winch, so winding the rope and pulling the attached mule to the wagon and train in the desired direction.

Not all went as planned and so the mule was permanently attached to a surplus old hopper wagon which was then placed in front of the train locomotive. The system was found to have several disadvantages, not least that it ran at walking pace, which for loading was ideal, but once a train had been completely loaded, it took ages to move it to a suitable siding. The 'rope' suffered from stretching, making the operator's calculations less precise, and the stopping of the mule not so exact. The stretched rope also occasionally snapped, either by wear and tear or if there was a 'snatch' in the movement. 'Rope' of course was something of a misnomer, to say the least; it was steel, several hundred yards long and nearly two inches thick.

The first remote controlled loco was delivered new in 1982, an 0-4-0 diesel hydraulic built in France by De Dietrich, No.89134. This is a white painted box on wheels with only a partial window to each end, a side door and ventilation panel. With the success of this remote controlled loco, Lafarge bought another four wheeled loco, this time from Italy. This came new to Barrow in 2005 and is resplendent in bright blue and white, with all round vision should there be a need for a driver. This 'Zephir' has a Rolls Royce engine, large rubber tyres for traction and, for rail guidance, a flanged bogie at each end which can be retracted. The white upper deck has blue painted handrails, with the lower blue panel relieved by a green band. The first remote loco was gradually run down after 1988, an ex- BR class 08 diesel shunter was taken on hire in 2008. This was No.08331, which also had the number H001. By early spring of 2009 a second Italian loco, similar to the first one, had been delivered.

Locomotives, Barrow-on-Soar
DIANE 0-4-0DH YE 2850 1961
BUNTY 0-4-0DM JF 4210018 1950 rebuilt TH 146c,1965
0-6-0DH TH 261V 1970's
NELLIE 4WDH ASEA OCO488 1982
D2324 0-6-0DM DC 2705 1961
RSH 8183 1961
040DH De Dietrich 89134 1988 new.
KILDARE 0-6-0DE YE 2741 1950s
IBURNDALE 0-6-0DE YE 2725 1958

Top. The fine Harringworth Viaduct over the river Welland in 2009, completed by the Midland Railway in 1880; 82 brick arches make it the longest viaduct in the UK. It is now a freight only line for aggregate trains leaving to the south-east.

Left. Redland Aggregates Self Discharge Train and Mountsorrel's rose tinted granite in 1995, showing the ease with which stone can be unloaded 'as required'. Ian Brown.

The Self Discharge Train in 2000 displaying its unique and cost effective method of rail ballast discharge on a track laying. The first four PGA wagons have emptied their stone via the continuous conveyor. Ian Brown.

PGA wagons at Redland Aggregates Harper Lane 'merry go round' depot in 1984; a bottom discharge facility, it is still in use and serves north London and Hertfordshire. Ian Brown.

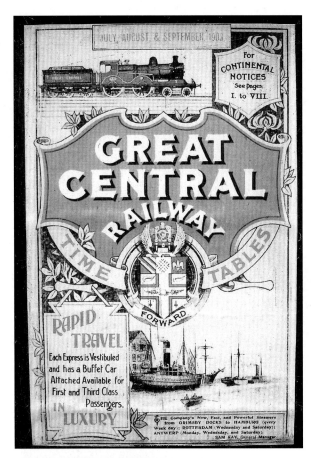

Left. Great Central Railway poster, dating from 1903, at Rothley station on the preserved Great Central Railway. The high standards of this preserved line echo the elegant days of the 1900s.

Below. Beautifully restored island platform and buildings, including covered staircase, at Rothley. 'Main line' trains now run through his fine GCR station once again.

Left. Navvies at work on a spoil tip near the Swithland Sidings in 1892 and the junction with the GCR. The new sleepers with grab handles make handling easier as the temporary track is moved around. Lafarge Aggregates.

CHLOE JADE 0-6-0DH RR 10212 1964
Scrapped 2009
08870 0-6-0DE Dar 1960
4WDH R/R Zephir 2005 new
4WDH R/R Zephir 2009 new
Both KILDARE and IBURNDALE were
ex-RMS Locotec Ltd
of Dewsbury, as was 08870; these locos
were returned to that company.
YE-Yorkshire Engine Co
    JF-John Fowler
    TH-Thomas Hill
    RSH-Robert Stephenson&Hawthorn
    Dar-British Railways, Darlington
    R/R-Rolls Royce
    DH-Diesel Hydraulic
    DM-Diesel Mechanical
    DE-Diesel Electric

Above. The western branch of the Mountsorrel Railway in April 2009; Nunkeley Hill Quarry is on the left, once served by a siding. The trackbed has been cleared by enthusiasts for the laying of new rails.

Below. Swithland Reservoir overflow control tower and dam in April 2009 which was built soon after the west branch of the Mountsorrel Railway opened, using stone from the quarries. Behind the trees are the Buddon Wood quarries which supplied roof slates for the St Pancras Hotel, the terminus in London of the Midland Railway.

So that all loaded trains can avoid the congested direct through line via Leicester used by express trains to and from London, they are routed via Syston Junction to Melton, Manton and Corby. They rejoin the slow line at Glendon Junction and run over Britain's longest viaduct of 82 brick arches, the Harringworth Viaduct over the river Welland and then southward.

A 37 wagon SDT train, the GL58 which departed from Barrow-on-Soar stone terminal at 21.19 hrs, destined for the Chelmsford depot, derailed on the approach to the River Great Ouse bridge, south of Ely, on Friday 22 June 2007, at 02.00 hrs. The train was hauled by No.60068 of DB Schenker, formerly an EWS locomotive. The fifteenth wagon derailed followed by a further ten and several ended up overhanging the lattice and box girder sections of the single track rail bridge. At least three wagons turned on their sides, and a further four were upturned on the twin box girder sections, discharging some 200 tonnes of aggregate into the river. The train was travelling south between

Top. **The Bond Lane approach to Mountsorrel (see Ordnance Survey) in characteristic fine stonework. It incorporates a stone plaque, 'M.G.C. 1919' (Mountsorrel Granite Company). Beyond it is the conveyor system in use today.**

Middle. **The Barrow-on-Soar loading point with Freightliner No.66604 hauling Network Rail bogie box wagons again in May 2009.**

Bottom. **The twin siding 'loading out' facility at Barrow-on-Soar in May 2009. Freightliner No.66612 has just arrived with empty Network Rail bogie box wagons in their bright yellow livery.**

Ely Dock Junction and Soham, about one mile south of Ely station. One section of the box girder bridge was distorted at the bearing end onto a pier in the river, caused by one wagon hanging precariously between the rails and its weight supported by the steel beam.

The removal of the derailed wagons was an extraordinary job, not completed until Thursday July 26 2007 over a month later. Three road cranes were used and a temporary road had to be built half a mile from the A142, with a stable stone platform made on the marshy ground. On the removal of the damaged wagons, dredging was put in hand so that local boating firms could resume their business. It is not often that a derailment disrupts *river* traffic! Several of the lesser damaged wagons were returned to Barrow-on-Soar terminal and placed on the cripple siding, where they remained for some ten months. Passengers requiring through journeys via Peterborough were advised to use the Ipswich to Cambridge services and Central Trains forward to Peterborough. A replacement bus service was introduced from Ely to Bury St Edmunds.

The rail Accident Investigation Branch (RAIB) was immediately advised and carried out an intensive survey to determine the cause of the derailment. Some two and a half years later the legal responsibility has not been established. As so often is the case with accidents, there is often not one single factor that can be deemed 'cause'. In this instance it has been suggested that broadly, perhaps, two factors, track and wheels, may have played a part. They usually do, after all. It is quite usual in accidents of course for small factors, each one harmless of itself, to combine at a critical time and with ill-luck, to bring about a derailment. Fortunately there were no injuries, and after some six months of intensive bridge rebuilding and track relaying, normal services were resumed.

Top. Freightliner No.66612 has just arrived from Syston Junction at the outer reception siding, adjacent to the main line, with 23 bogie box wagons, 10A(E) with a capacity of 77.3 tonnes each.

Middle. A 2009 general view looking south towards Leicester. In the reception siding is a Freightliner with Network Rail yellow box wagons. On the left the 'Italian' job, the Zephir, is propelling similar wagons through the loading point. On the right are PGA wagons on the Wabtec repair siding.

Bottom. 2009 again with the Zephir remote controlled shunting loco with Freightliner No.66604 at the head of its wagons in No.2 road. In the distance another Class 66 awaits its turn for loading.

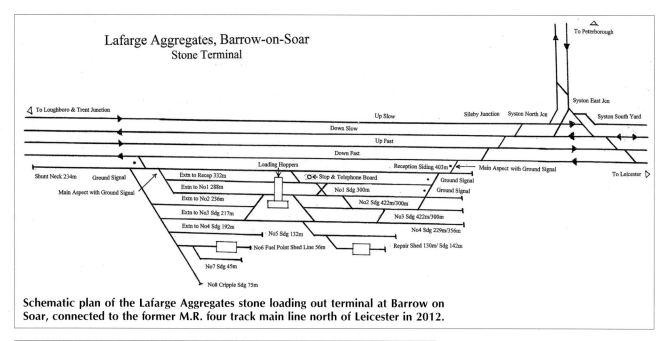

Lafarge Aggregates, Barrow-on-Soar
Stone Terminal

Schematic plan of the Lafarge Aggregates stone loading out terminal at Barrow on Soar, connected to the former M.R. four track main line north of Leicester in 2012.

Left. The strange box-like French-built 1961 'Dietrix' remote controlled loco amongst Lafarge Aggregates PGA wagons at Barrow-on-Soar; it would hardly win any prizes for best looking locomotive.

Below. Redland Aggregates liveried 'Nelly', ASEA No.OCO488 built in 1982, receiving minor attention in 1991. The small fifth wheel just visible was used to input speed, distance and direction details to the on-board computer. Sydney A. Leleux.

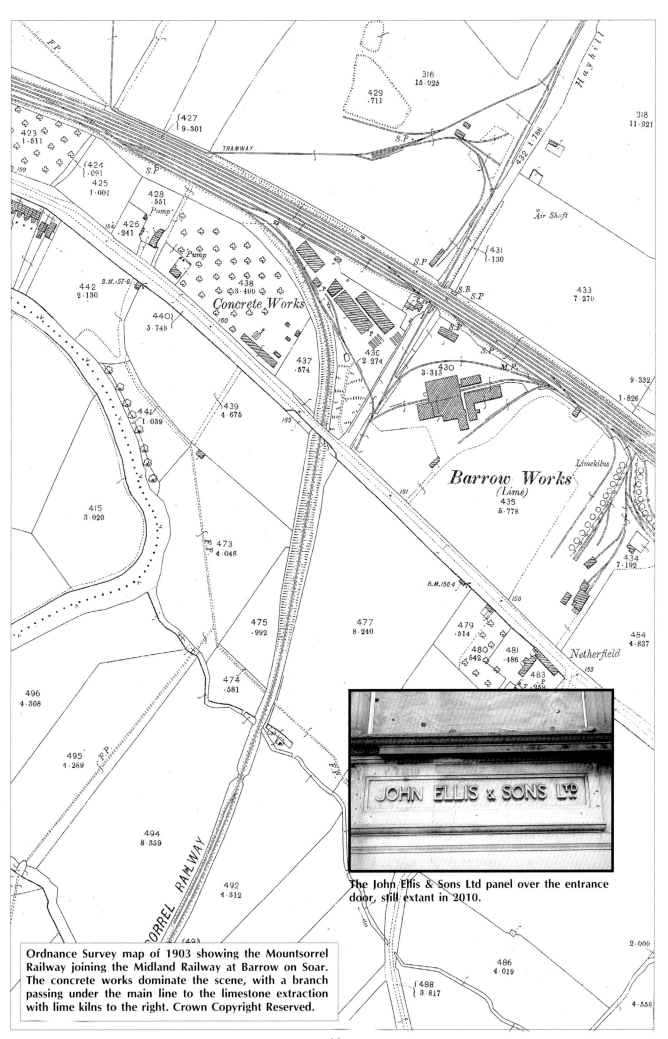

The John Ellis & Sons Ltd panel over the entrance door, still extant in 2010.

Ordnance Survey map of 1903 showing the Mountsorrel Railway joining the Midland Railway at Barrow on Soar. The concrete works dominate the scene, with a branch passing under the main line to the limestone extraction with lime kilns to the right. Crown Copyright Reserved.

Right. No.2 loading point siding (though it is hardly necessary to point this out!) discharging 77 tonnes into a bogie box wagon controlled by the operator in the high level cabin in May 2009. Through the steelwork can be seen the Italian remote controlled Zephir loco.

Top. The original enamel gable sign of Joseph Ellis & Sons Ltd, now at the GCR's preserved Rothley station in April 2009.

Middle. One of Joseph Ellis & Sons Ltd local offices, transplanted to the Great Central Railway at Rothley and now serving as a tea room in 2009.

Bottom. Aerial view in 1930 of the extensive John Ellis & Sons Barrow-on-Soar concrete works beside the four track ex-Midland Railway main line, looking north. Sidings proliferate around the vast site. Collection Andrew Moore.

50

Looking north from the railway control cabin roof, with the four track main line to the right. Lafarge PGA wagons surround the Freightliner class 66 in its refuelling shed. The former rail connection to the quarry curved in from the left where the wagons are stored. All views were taken in May 2009.

Inside the control cabin. The operator can discharge a precise volume of stone to each wagon, and controls the remote shunting loco too.

Busy scene in 2009 at Barrow Stone Terminal, with Lafarge and Redland PGA wagons predominating. On the right is the six wheel Rolls Royce loco, 'Chloe Jade' and beyond it the cripple siding and repair shed. On the left across the tracks are the modern lime works, once served by rail.

At the end of the Self Discharge Train we have the swivel action conveyor discharge wagon with its inclined elevator, to place stone precisely where it is wanted. Behind it is the PGA power wagon.

Top. The power PGA wagon, showing the conveyor belt which links all the other wagons in the train in May 2009.

Middle. Lafarge Aggregates PGA wagon built by the Standard Wagon Company in 1978 for Redland Aggregates, taken over in 1997; this is one of 40 built, with a gross laden weight of 51 tonnes.

Bottom. Two trains of newly-built Network Rail bogie box wagons, ready for positioning at loading points one and two. Two Self Discharge Trains await loading in the distance and there are five PGAs on the repair siding. The remote Zephir is mutely propelling box wagons to the loader.

Above left. Newly painted Redland Aggregate PGA wagons at Barrow stone loading terminal in 2009, the controllers high level cabin affording a clear view of all the activities. Ian Brown.

Above right. An early Redland Aggregates livery was pale green for body and solebar with REDLAND in, naturally, red. The later livery included AGGREGATES in white on a dark blue panel with the solebar in blue. Ian Brown.

The unfortunate accident in June 2007 when the Lafarge Aggregates Self Discharge Train destined for Chelmsford, hauled by DB Schenker No.60068, was partially derailed on the River Great Ouse bridge, one mile south of Ely station. A worse place to de-rail is hard to imagine – see text.

Stone squarers sheds and vast piles of granite setts in the 1920s with interwoven sidings. The Lanes Hill and Top Pit quarries at Stoney Stanton are on the left. Keith Robertson.

4. STONEY STANTON QUARRY

The village of Stoney Stanton and its sister, Sapcote, lie between the Roman road, the Fosse Way to the south, and to the north by the gently winding old LNWR main line between Birmingham and Leicester. They sit seven miles along this line from Wigston South Junction, Leicester. Stoney Stanton Parish Council had its own 'Parish Pit' as early as 1800, for filling in the potholes on local roads. The population was largely engaged in agriculture with a few hosiery outworkers. In 1871 the population was 681, rising in the next ten years to 995; by 1911 there were 1,539 people shown in the census. This growth came from new jobs, as the hosiery trade and the local stone quarrying went from strength to strength. The early Parish Pit quarry, later to be known as Carey Hill Road quarry, expanded such that the village became 'carved out' by several workings close by the houses. Quarrying was thirsty work; in Carey Hill Road there was the Bull's Head, and near the entrance to the recent Clint Hill Drive the Blue Bell. The Frank's Arms in Church Street disappeared as the Clint Hill quarry grew, with the Star Inn near Church Walk swallowed up by Little Pit or Hall Close Quarry.

In the 1870s the Mountsorrel Granite Co acquired Little Pit and Clint Hill Quarries, and quite possibly this was through the efforts of the Reverend John Martin, rector of the Parish between 1875 and 1879. He was related to the Martin family who had leased the Mountsorrel Quarry from Lord Lanesborough. Parish Pit was sold for £3,000 and upon purchase of Clint Hill quarry, it was made deeper, so a derrick crane was installed to lift rail wagons from the bottom levels up to a stone crushing plant. A short tunnel under New Road was made to get easier access to Carey Hill quarry, which had been originally owned by William Hewitt, whose local nickname was 'Billy Whip'. This was on account of his men who used whipping hammers to make setts; his residence, 'Sett House' in Broughton Road was indeed built of them. A vertical hoist was erected, replacing the derrick crane, to raise railway wagons from a depth of 180 feet; a pump house was required and this also brought pure water to fifteen taps within the village. Little Pit (called

Hall Close on the Ordnance Survey extract) beside St Michael's Church was backfilled and made into allotment gardens in 1911. Landfill in this country is nothing new.

The Mountsorrel Granite Co bought Walkers Home Farm and land off the road between Stoney Stanton and Sapcote, to the north, and commenced stone extraction at what was known as Top Pit or Top Quarry, cut into the northern slopes of Mill Hill. The company also took over the adjacent Lanes Hill quarry. A crushing plant was erected on the level at Top Quarry and a 'Blondin' aerial ropeway erected to connect the lower extractive areas with the crusher and sett making sheds. Clint Hill quarry, the most northerly in the village, was filled with water during the Great War, 1914-18 but was pumped out after the war and reopened, finally closing in 1921. Both Top Pit and Granitethorpe, or Sapcote Quarry, south of Stoney Stanton, had a hand-worked narrow gauge railway. Top Pit, despite its size and two levels of working faces, had only one short section of track, from the working faces to the sett sheds and crushing plant with

Stoney Stanton Quarry in the 1920s, showing several working benches, with the lower level covered in temporary tracks which fan out to each work station. Overhead is an aerial ropeway, or 'Blondin' which many quarries used. Noel Wakeling.

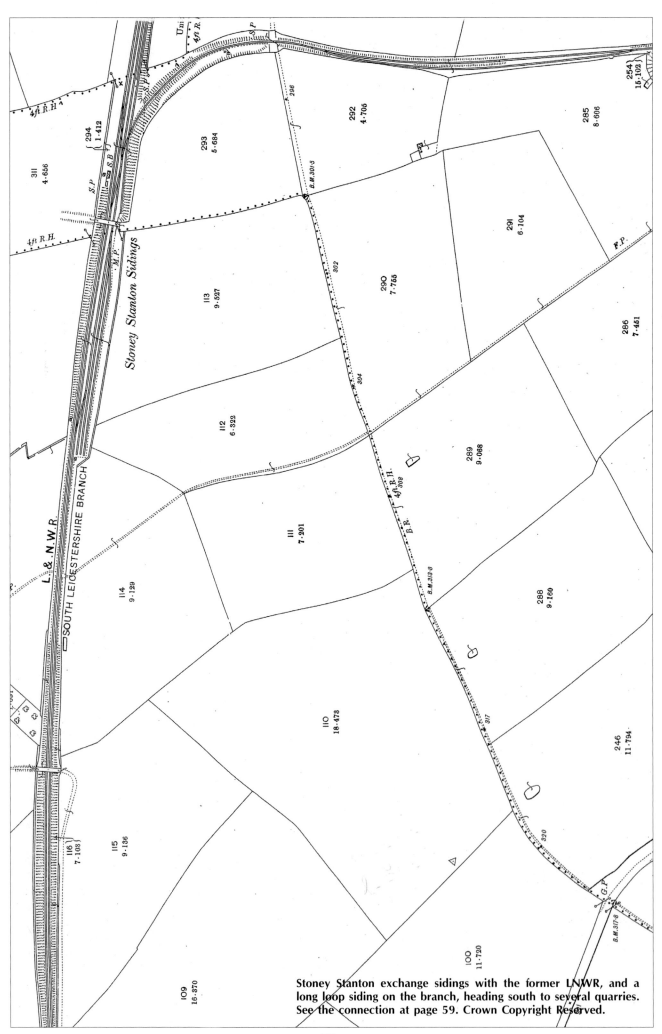

Stoney Stanton exchange sidings with the former LNWR, and a
long loop siding on the branch, heading south to several quarries.
See the connection at page 59. Crown Copyright Reserved.

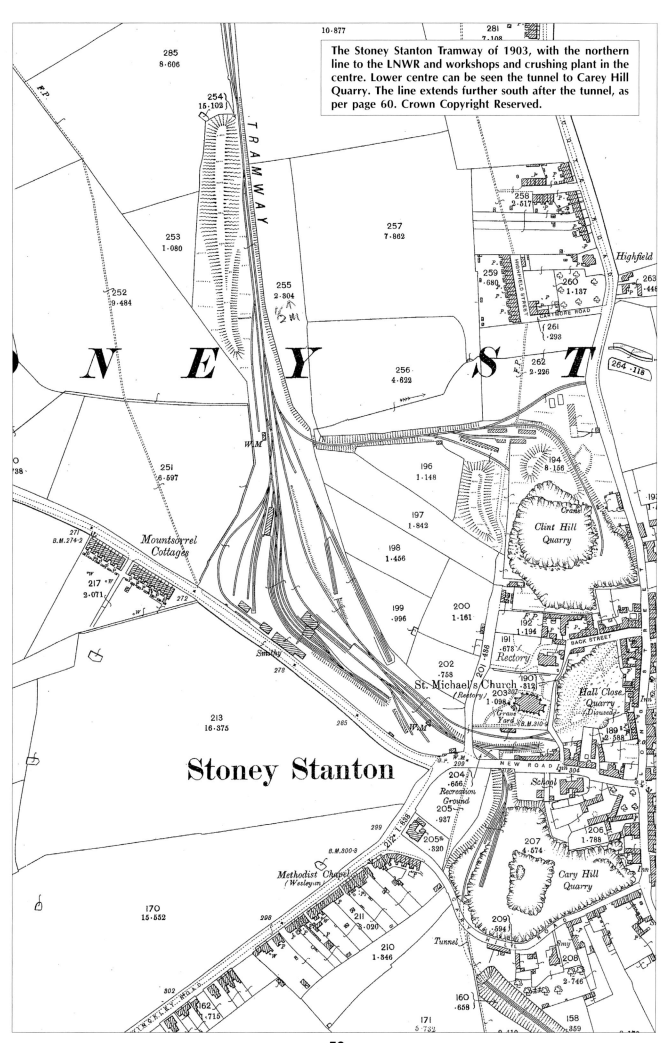

The Stoney Stanton Tramway of 1903, with the northern line to the LNWR and workshops and crushing plant in the centre. Lower centre can be seen the tunnel to Carey Hill Quarry. The line extends further south after the tunnel, as per page 60. Crown Copyright Reserved.

Stoney Stanton

Mountsorrel Cottages

Clint Hill Quarry

St. Michael's Church

Hall Close Quarry (Disused)

Rectory

Grave Yard

Recreation Ground

Methodist Chapel (Wesleyan)

Cary Hill Quarry

Tunnel

School

Highfield

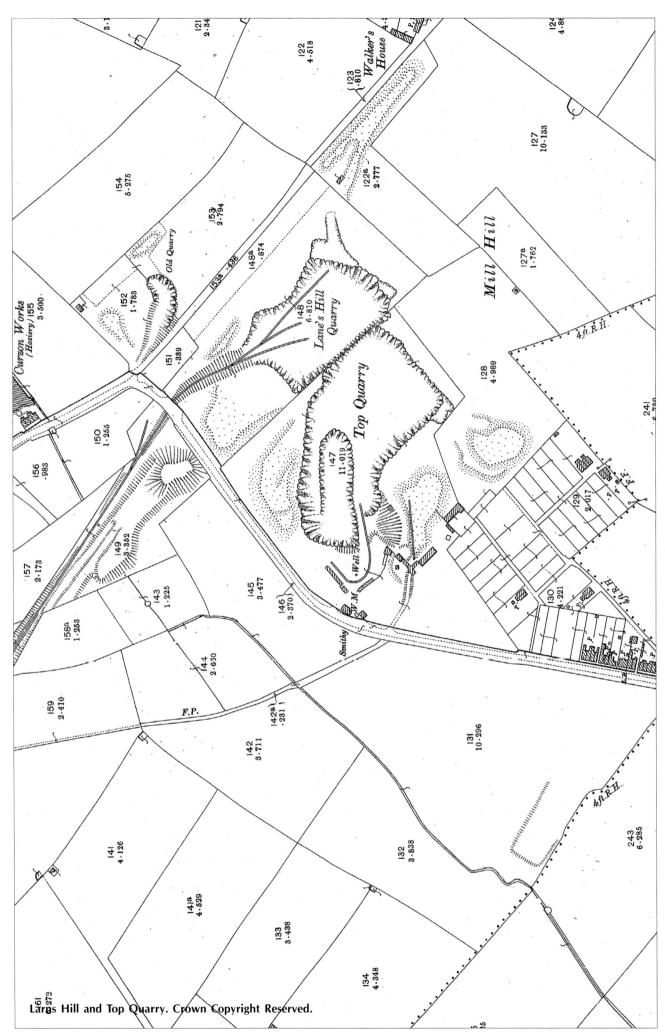

Lanes Hill and Top Quarry. Crown Copyright Reserved.

ROBBIE with attendants in 1910, showing off the polished brass and paintwork. The young man at left may well be the diarist W.F. Martin. Alison Jackson.

a separate short length for the spoil tip. Granitethorpe had an inclined single track from the heart of the working area, terminating in a wagon turntable with a 90 degree turn to a long spur serving the sheds and works. A short spur from this turntable terminated at a second wagon turning point with a short siding off it. At first all the stone items produced were transported by horse and cart; later steam road waggons were used.

The methods of stone extraction was firstly to remove the overburden which often included random and poor quality, very weathered stone. Drilling for blasting meant a row of holes, one to six feet from the cliff edge and between 12 and 15 feet deep. These were charged with explosive and fired; as the pit depths got greater, as many as 48 charges on one face were made to bring down thousands of tons in the one blast. The extra large boulders had to be laboriously hammered and chiselled, though later developments in explosives, including the use of 'ammonal' (ammonia nitrate and aluminium) enabled such blocks to be tackled with greater safety.

A Private Siding Agreement (PSA) was made between the LNWR and the Mountsorrel Granite Co, dated 12th November 1878, for three sidings to the south side of the main line, with a signal box controlling all movements at the junction. By 1903 these were known as Stoney Stanton Sidings, and were later

supplemented by two more sidings, to the east of the junction. The signal box was situated opposite the mineral branch junction which diverged at right angles and headed south, the junction from the mineral branch being controlled by a home signal inside the quarry company's boundary. A short distance down the branch was a 300 yard loop siding. About half a mile from the junction another very long loop siding then split into a series of sidings, with one turning east on an embankment to Clint Hill Quarry and its several stone setters sheds and a further three sidings. The 'main line' of the mineral railway then had six sidings into the crushing and tar macadam plant, overlooked by terraces for quarrymen, 'Mountsorrel Cottages'.

The numerous sidings entered the village from the west side, passing under the quaintly-named Knock Verges road and then into Hall Close Quarry which had fallen out of use by 1887. A single track curved south under New Road with three sidings branching off into Carey Hill Quarry, which had a single track incline built in 1897. The main line continued in an 'S' curve at the south side of Carey Hill quarry and then tunnelled under Carey Hill road for some distance. The curved tunnel was over a hundred yards long with its southern portal in a very deep (forty feet or so) cutting. This track then headed straight for about 500 yards where it passed under the Sapcote Road;

it then entered a cutting which opened out into the Lanes Hill Quarry, with its three sidings. The tunnel was driven by the quarry men in 1885, who also laid the connecting railway tracks.

With the increasing development of the Stoney Stanton quarries under the Martin ownership, there was very close daily integration with the Mounsorrel business. This is evident from the diaries of W.F. Martin, the grandson of William John Martin who had acquired that business from a Mr Jackson in 1850. Initially wooden dumb buffered wagons of end-tipping 'contractors type' were used, horse drawn. Steam locomotives came to Stoney Stanton in 1890 with the delivery new from Hunslet of 0-4-0ST No.507, named CHARLIE. No.856 WALTER was delivered in 1892 and then No.669 of 1898 THE EARL, No.856 ROBBIE in 1904 and then No.955 GERALD, built in 1907. The transfer of locomotives between quarries was common, as noted in the previous chapter and No.1146 VIOLET of 1913 duly arrived from Mountsorrel in May 1935. THE COUNTESS, No.670 of 1898, was moved from the Enderby Quarries, having earlier transferred there from Mountsorrel. THE CHAIRMAN, an 0-4-0 diesel mechanical Ruston Hornsby No.237921 built in 1946, was moved from the Mountsorrel Tar Macadam Co Ltd in 1948, and was moved for a second time to Enderby in November 1956. BUNTY, another 0-4-0 diesel mechanical, this time built by John Fowler,

The tar macadam plant at Stoney Stanton in August 1923, towering over the several sidings with their loaded wagons awaiting dispatch. Lafarge Aggregates.

No.4210018, was delivered new in 1950 to Stoney Stanton. An unnamed 0-4-0 diesel mechanical from Baguley, No.3006 of 1937, was transferred 'across the tracks' from the Potters Marston Concrete Works (to the north of the main line, about half a mile east of the Stoney Stanton junction) of John Ellis & Sons Ltd. This was scrapped early in 1958. The livery of the steam locomotives was black with a double fine red coach painted lining, with all brass and copper fittings highly polished. The total length of the Stoney Stanton Mineral Railway, from the junction at the exchange sidings to the farthest point south in Lanes Hill Quarry, was one mile and thirty chains, something under a mile and a half. In the heyday of this intensive quarrying in the village, there were some thirty men working in both Clint Hill and the Carey Hill quarries. A photograph shows 21 sett makers In 1900 with their foreman, Tom Robertson, whose father was also a sett maker. The Robertson family still reside in the village with one member still at work in a local quarry. The largest number of men and boys who worked within the group of quarries in the village was 190. The Stoney Stanton quarries and the Enderby quarries were amalgamated into the Enderby & Stoney Stanton Granite Co Ltd, Incorporated on 30th November 1894. Private owner open wagons were in use and the joint ownership name was applied from around this time. Some no doubt were re-painted wagons from the fleet at Enderby. Both three and six plank wagons acquired this new livery, adverts to promote the joint company's products. At least one of these wagons was still on site in 1955, in a run-down condition but with partial livery fragments remaining. This suggests that it had been used for internal use only. It is understood that many of the private owner wagons for the two quarry companies were built at Stoney Stanton, at the firm's wagon works on the long 'L' shaped boundary siding to the west, which terminated opposite the Mountsorrel Cottages.

Cary Hill Quarry viewed from an aeroplane in 1923, demonstrating the dizzy proximity of houses all around the sides. Centre left, the near vertical wagon hoist brought up loaded wagons to be taken away on the 'S' curved siding near the top. Lafarge Aggregates.

Aerial view in 1923 looking north to the LNWR main line, with the Stoney Stanton railway connecting track heading towards the double exchange sidings. On the left are the wagon repair workshops, with in middle distance behind the row of trees, the branch to the Clint Hill Quarry. Lafarge Aggregates.

Stoney Stanton Quarry and its village houses close by in 1900. In the foreground are piles of prepared road setts ready for dispatch on the railway. Alison Jackson.

Lanes Hill or Top Pit Quarry again in 1910. Formerly two separate quarries which were blasted through to make one single more economical operation. A fan of narrow gauge sidings occupy the newer, deeper pit, with an aerial ropeway above. Alison Jackson.

A beautiful 'O' gauge model of wagon No.426, a 10 ton capacity wagon in bauxite livery with black shadow to white letters, made and photographed by David Webb.

Aerial view of Carey Hill Quarry with the rail tunnel and wagon hoist on the left passing under New Street, with St.Michael's Church in Stoney Stanton village.

The heart of Earl Shilton Quarry, dominated by the aerial ropeway tower and its concrete base in 1920. Two narrow gauge steam locos are engaged in shunting the endless rakes of road setts. Andrew Moore.

5. EARL SHILTON QUARRY

Only some five hundred yards to the east of Stoney Stanton Sidings, on the north side of the main line, were further exchange sidings and a short branch line, put there to serve the Earl Shilton Quarry. Known as New Shilton Sidings, they were installed under an Agreement dated 22nd March 1901. There was a 36 lever signal box at the north side of the main line, opposite the Stoney Stanton Sidings. It had under its control the 'up' sidings ground frame for the New Shilton Sidings.

A single siding curved northward in a shallow cutting, rising on a gentle gradient and soon terminated at an exchange platform where the internal narrow gauge system was able to transfer stone to standard gauge wagons. The arrangements for exchange consisted of three standard gauge sidings with catch points to protect the main line. At a later date, just inside the boundary gate, a turnout was laid so that a circular loop was formed around the now developing site, which became a cement products factory. At the northern limit of this siding, a seventy-five yard passing loop was put in; this arrangement of loops was still in place in 1963.

From the interchange platform, a 2ft gauge system headed north for about three quarters of a mile curving through fields and crossing over a small stream before its approach to a farm called The Yennards. Here it terminated in two loop sidings and an overhead crushing, sieving and loading plant. The associated quarries, called Barrow Hill, were made up of two separate workings. The southern-most one lay by the farm, The Yennards and was known as No.1 Pit, while the adjacent north quarry was known as Barrow Hill or No.2 Pit. A track led off from The Yennards to the No.2 Pit where there was a 'Blondin' overhead ropeway, terminating at the crushing plant. This sloped down into the depths of the quarry and brought out rough stone in steel buckets to be tipped at high level into storage bins. At The Yennards works there was a complex and intricate rail system which transferred wagons from the Blondin to sett makers sheds and stockpiles. It might be wondered that neither of these sites involved the name 'Earl Shilton'; in fact it took the name from the nearest village to the west.

It would appear that, probably from the outset of quarrying at Earl Shilton, ownership was vested in the Stoney Stanton Granite Co, later incorporated with the Enderby Quarry. With the demise of granite setts for road making in the 1930s, the concrete products business of John Ellis & Sons Ltd was established on the site nearest the main line, convenient for rail access. Concrete production at Barrow-on-Soar was transferred to this new site, called Potters Marston after the Parish, in 1937. At its peak in 1955 this concrete manufactory produced 35,000 tons of assorted concrete products, much of it sent out by rail from the sidings. A narrow gauge railway operated in the works for the movement of all manner of items, many of them large and heavy. This was a simple north-south alignment with a bisecting X siding; at the southern tip was an interchange dock to the standard gauge circular siding. Two other north-south spurs served the numerous production buildings, most of which had access to the railway. Production ceased in 1980, with the site eventually sold; it is now in use as a Calor Gas Depot. The narrow gauge tracks were taken out of use in 1957.

****

The earliest motive power for the Earl Shilton Quarry railway was an 0-4-0 well tank of German antecedents, transferred from the similar narrow gauge railway at Enderby Quarry. There has been much conjecture as to the builder of this locomotive; it is presumed to be an Orenstein & Koppel design but like some problems in archaeology it has influences of more than one maker. It has been suggested that it may have been built by Borsig under contract, hence the variation in detail in its regulator valve and the wheel balance weights. It was named CHESHAM which at least suggests a former place of work, possibly by a contractor.

A rare picture of the isolated Earl Shilton Quarry in 1910 showing the aerial ropeway strung across a deeper pit, with two rail sidings on a former bench probably served by the ropeway too. Alison Jackson.

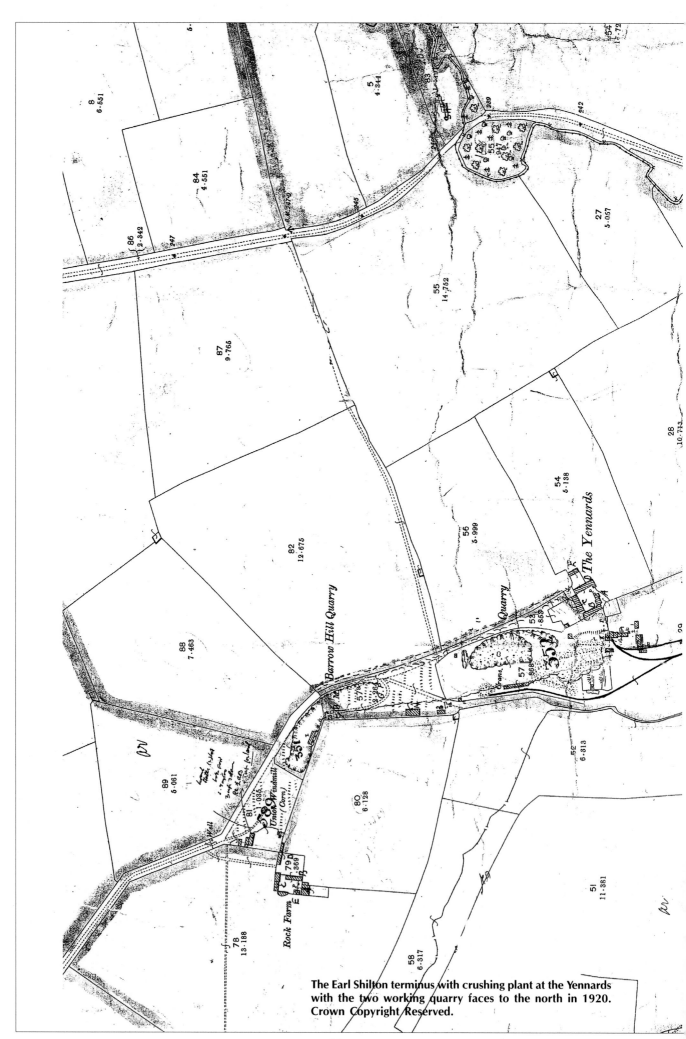

The Earl Shilton terminus with crushing plant at the Yennards with the two working quarry faces to the north in 1920. Crown Copyright Reserved.

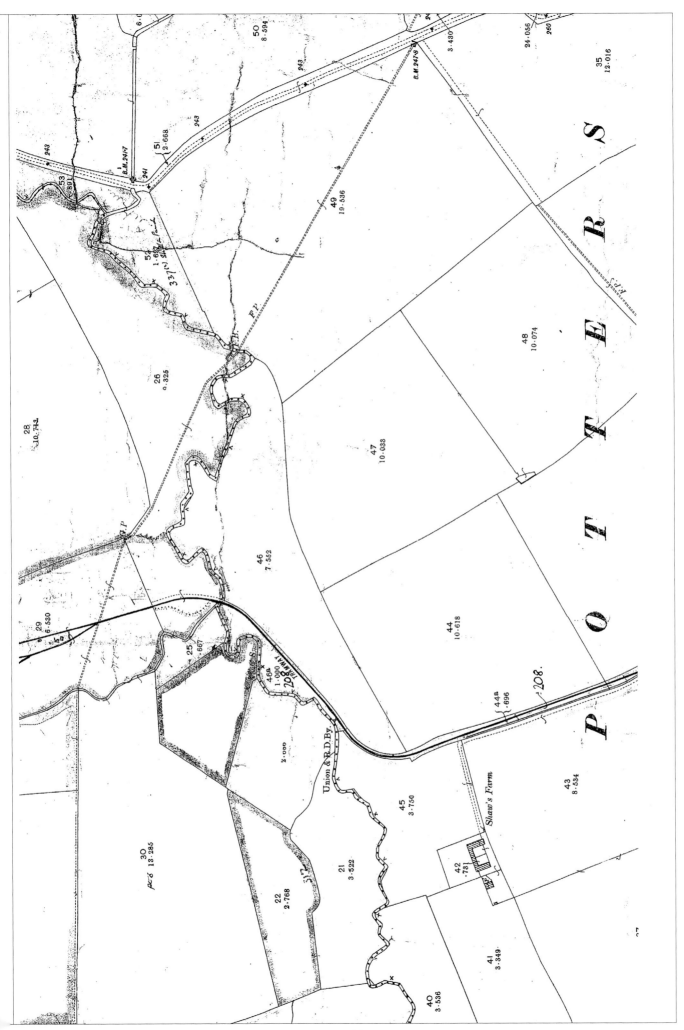

The BARON in a somewhat expanded water colour version of the scene on page 33.

Four Bagnall 0-4-0STs were also transferred from Enderby; Nos.1592 and 1618 of 1900 and Nos.1659 and 1660 of 1901. These were later to be transferred to Huncote Quarry, probably over several years during the 1930s. The locos had names with military associations though the first was a nickname (of the Earl Roberts) and the second is obscure. They were: BOBS, LESTER, BULLER and KITCHENER.

An 0-4-0 diesel mechanical built by Baguley of Burton on Trent, No.3006, was delivered new in 1937. It was transferred away to Stoney Stanton granite quarry in 1952, after which a steam crane carried out the shunting.

Earl Shilton Quarry received three new locos, this time from Ransomes & Rapier of Ipswich, all diesel mechanical 0-4-0s, Nos.69 and 75 built in 1936 and No.81 of 1938. No.69 went on to Huncote Quarry around 1938, No.75 was sold to Berry's of Leicester for scrap in October 1957 and No.81 was scrapped on site. Two Ruston & Hornsby diesel mechanical 0-4-0s, built in 1937, came from the dealer Pugsley in early 1950, Nos.187089 and 189941. They were disposed of with Berry's in late 1957. Another arrival in 1950 was an 0-4-0 petrol mechanical built by Motor Rail in 1932, bought from R.R. Paton Ltd; a dealer in Cardiff; it too finished its days with Berry's scrap merchant, in October 1957. This effectively saw the closing down the Earl Shilton quarrying operation. The standard gauge peripheral railway to the John Ellis & Sons business required motive power, and it is understood that a locomotive and steam crane were loaned from the Stoney Stanton Quarry, 'down the tracks'. It is not clear as to when this standard gauge line went out of use, but the controlling signal box was closed on 24th April, 1964, so around this date is the most likely time; certainly the internal sidings were shown on the Ordnance Survey maps in 1963.

Above. In the left distance is the site of the Stoney Stanton Sidings and nearer the camera, right foreground, the exchange sidings to Earl Shilton Quarry in April 2009.

Below. A boundary gate by the Leicester-Hinkley main line in 2009 where the spur from the exchange sidings left the LNWR to enter Earl Shilton Quarry works, later occupied by the John Ellis concrete works.

Below. The German-built 0-4-0 well tank loco CHESHAM at the exchange platform about 1910 with standard gauge private wagons from the local colliery at Moira. Collection Frank Jones.

The vertical wagon hoist and its supporting platform with stone abutments in 1879. A small steel tub wagon under the top wheel tripod is about to be sent on its way to the crusher. Andrew Moore.

6. HUNCOTE QUARRY.
With Narborough and Red Hill Quarries.

Of the several stone quarries in Leicestershire, Huncote Quarry was the most charmingly situated, between Huncote and Croft villages, to the west of Leicester, in rolling countryside with a tinkling stream. In this sylvan setting, the quarry had its own narrow gauge railway winding through cow pastures on its way to the standard gauge mineral branch line at Narborough.

Stone had been extracted from Croft Hill (summit 420ft and thus something of a local height) since 1797 and was used in local buildings, to repair Enderby church and in the local roads. The Earl of Stamford and Warrington was the Lord of the Manor of Huncote, which in 1840 consisted of 900 acres. Both the Everard and Ellis families were also land owners. By 1880 Huncote Village was a thriving place, with the Barley Sheaf pub and the Red Lion in the centre of the village. Behind the Red Lion was Needham's Brewery between Coley's Yard and the Workhouse Yard. There was a malthouse on the slopes of Mount Pleasant facing the Red Lion pub. There were three bakehouses in the village and Huncote Mill astride the Thurlastone Brook, where John Hobill was the miller in the mid-19th century. The local blacksmith in 1866 was James West who sharpened the quarry drills and carried out general repairs for the quarry owners.

It is apparent that, in the early days of stone quarrying, there were several owners, the account books for 1848-50 showing that a William Smith from Groby was operating at Huncote. In the year 1853, evidently, only 431 tons were

sold. In March 1866 George Marston acquired the Huncote Quarry at the age of 39. He lived at 'The Cedars' in Broad Street, Enderby, and was described as a 'Granite Merchant' in 1881. There were several quarries at Enderby, owned by the Marston family or the Rawson family (see section on Enderby Quarry). The census of 1871 showed that of the 223 souls in Huncote, 24 were quarrymen.

Huncote Quarry was cut into the north-eastern slopes of Croft Hill, with Bridge Street from Huncote forming the northern extremity. To the east, the confines were marked by a substantial farm track still used to this day, which runs at the base of the reconstituted Croft Hill, formed of spoil from Croft Quarry which was backfilled into the old Huncote Quarry on its closure. The stone extracted was granite-diorite and even by 1877 the working was being carried out at two distinct levels. The heyday of Huncote was from 1871 to 1939, when there were as many as one hundred men working; forty were labourers knocking-up the large blasted boulders, and the rest loaded up the stone into carts and later into the railway wagons. The drillers worked on the stone faces suspended on ropes. The sizes of road setts made were 3 x 5, 4 x 4 and 4 x 5 inches; they were loaded into horse drawn carts and taken to Narborough station.

Under the ownership of George Marston the quarry was expanded and soon became a part of the larger trading group Enderby & Stoney Stanton Granite Quarries Ltd. It is not clear when a narrow gauge railway was first laid, but it probably was around 1900.

Certainly the tramway was well established by 1916. A double track incline some 50 yards in length rose from one side of the square shaped quarry and then split with several sidings to both sides of two long sett making sheds. This incline replaced a timber vertical hoist which lifted wagons from the depths, which had been in use as late as 1877. Another branch of the narrow gauge railway had a loop which connected with the stone setters siding and a spoil tip spur. From the crushing plant a 'Y' junction was formed with a short central spur to the locomotive shed, with the eastern branch running round a spoil tip; this branch had a loop nearest the farm track previously mentioned and passed over it on the level and then formed the 'main line'.

From this level crossing the line then headed east across a field on a low embankment, until it approached the Thurlaston Brook, where there were four arches to permit flood water relief. The line crossed the river on a two span steel girder bridge on concrete abutments, continuing on the other side on an embankment around Huncote village outskirts. Due to the light construction of this bridge, there was a weight limit of 20 tons, and this restricted the steam hauled trains to ten skip wagons in the latter days. The line then continued in a straight line through fields to a shallow cutting, crossed by a farm track bridge (still in-situ). There followed a 90 degree turn to the north with a deepening cutting where it passed under the Huncote Road bridge; its elaborate portals are still visible, beside the Croft View Cottages.

Two foot gauge stalwart BULLER, Bagnall No.1659 of 1901, resting between jobs on the Huncote Railway in the 1930s. G. Alliez.

73

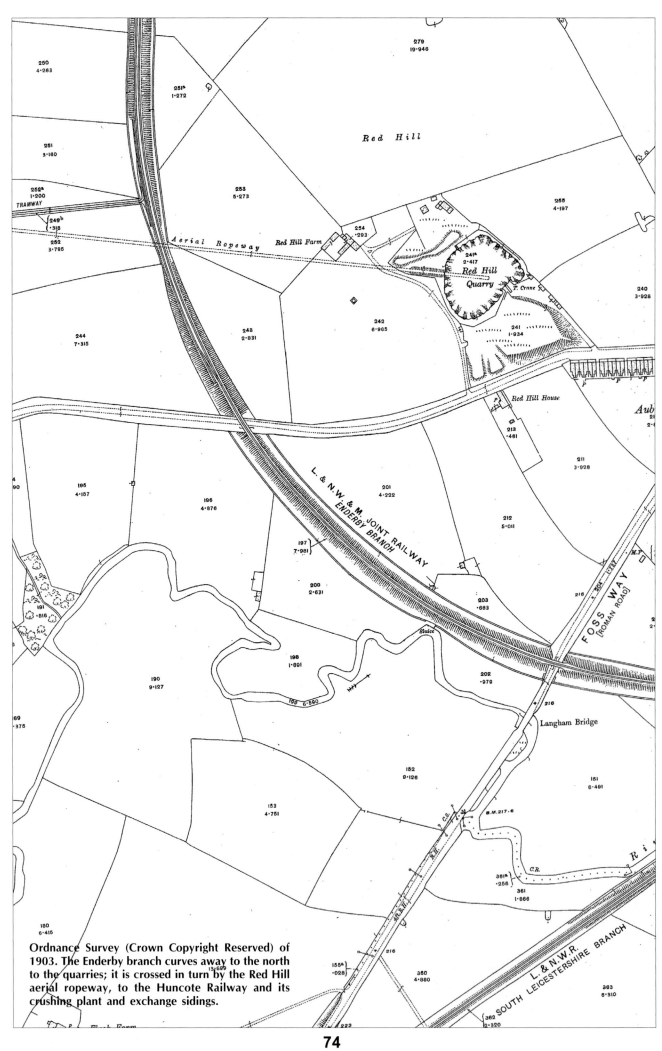

Ordnance Survey (Crown Copyright Reserved) of 1903. The Enderby branch curves away to the north to the quarries; it is crossed in turn by the Red Hill aerial ropeway, to the Huncote Railway and its crushing plant and exchange sidings.

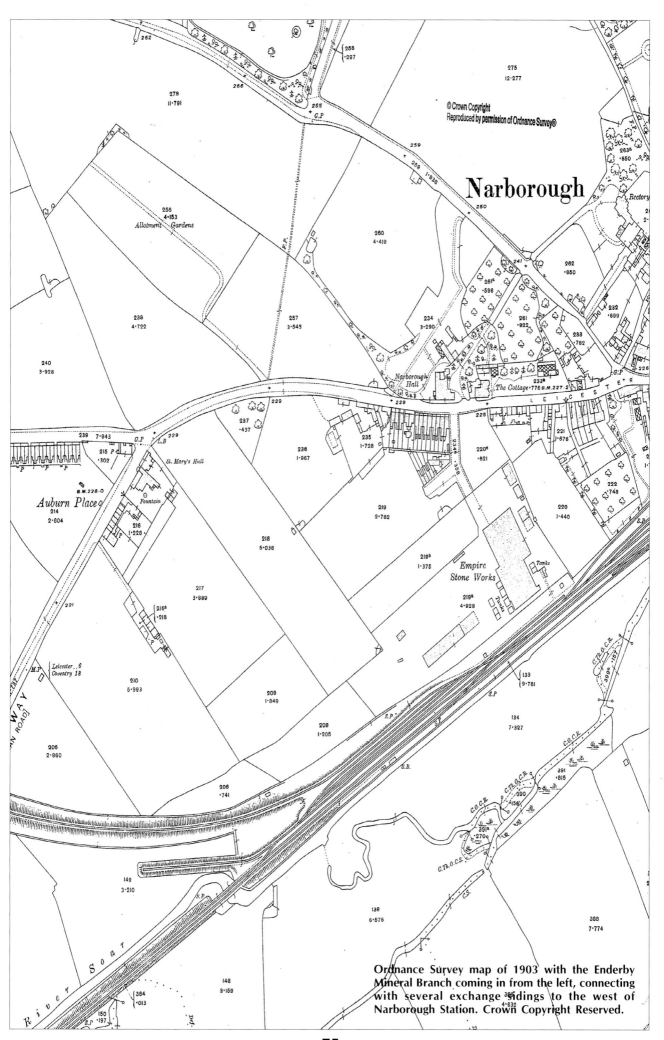

Ordnance Survey map of 1903 with the Enderby Mineral Branch coming in from the left, connecting with several exchange sidings to the west of Narborough Station. Crown Copyright Reserved.

After the bridge the line then curved east, passing spoil tips from the Narborough Quarry, now a small hill covered with surface pipework to extract methane gases; the former quarry has been backfilled with refuse. When working, Narborough Quarry was another to make use of the 'Blondin' aerial ropeway system, as there was a crushing plant here which also took stone for processing from the Red Hill Quarry, in the hill opposite. Once isolated, the Red Hill Quarry is now in a built up residential part of Narborough.

The Huncote Railway split into several sidings within the plant and continued in a loop serving a long shed for squarers. From the crushing plant, a double track shallow incline rose up the hill for 250 yards, where it divided into a 'T' with the two arms running along on the top of a concrete loading dock. This platform, 140 yards in length was built on the joint LNWR/MR Enderby mineral branch as an exchange point, from the narrow gauge to standard gauge wagons. This was a long loop siding of some 450 yards, with catch points at each end to protect the single track line.

Another 'Blondin' aerial ropeway crossed this branch, terminating at the Red Hill Quarry. This was some 700 yards long and at a later date wire netting was slung beneath it, to ensure that no stones fell on the track. The Enderby branch had a long sweeping curve from this loading platform, heading south so that it joined the LNWR South Leicester main line at

exchange sidings to the north-west side of Narborough Station. The remaining north section of this branch is described in the section on Enderby Quarry.

With the Earl Shilton, Huncote, Narborough and Red Hill Quarries were all in the same ownership (the Marston family) unsurprisingly there were several transfers of locomotives over the years. More followed and with the grouping together of the Enderby and Stoney Stanton Quarries, four Bagnall locomotives which had worked on the Enderby narrow gauge system were sent to work at the Earl Shilton quarry; later they were sent to Huncote, which would have meant that they were also shunting at the Narborough works.

The Red Hill Quarry also had a 2ft gauge system within the small quarry, but this was hand worked. Wagons from the quarry would serve to fill buckets on the aerial ropeway, powered by a steam boiler. Local tradition has it that the Red Hill quarry closed around 1917, as it was the habit of the boiler man to nip off to one of the local pubs at lunch time. He evidently tied a stone onto the boilers safety valve, and with a delayed return to work, the boiler had exploded! It also powered the Blondin and the winch to the Narborough incline to the transfer dock and as the expense of renewal was prohibitive, it was all closed down. The fate of the wretched boiler man is unrecorded.

The four Bagnall 0-4-0STs, BOBS, LESTER, BULLER and KITCHENER were described in the previous chapter. In 1926 a four wheeled petrol engine loco built by Muir Hill was delivered

new to Huncote, No.3. Ransomes & Rapier diesel mechanical 0-4-0 No.69, also mentioned in the previous chapter, came from Earl Shilton. Neither of these two diesels carried names and their disposal is unknown.

During the last war only a few men were working at Huncote, producing crushed stone for use on roads and more importantly, for building and repairs to airfields. Huncote was closed soon after the war as was Narborough, both making use of road transport after the demise of the railway. The business was acquired by Redland Aggregates Ltd in 1951 and closed. A subsidiary, Redland Purle, apparently carried out the backfilling of Narborough. Quarry.

Above. **A portrait of Bagnall LESTER of 1900 in 1930; it kept company with fellow General BULLER. G. Alliez.**

The solidly built stone parapets to the Huncote Road bridge over the Huncote Railway, near Hill View cottages on the outskirts of Huncote village in April 2009. The quarry was to the left via a cutting, with Narborough interchange and works over to the right.

Tree-tangled remnants of the low embankment and its ruined culverts built to relieve flooding on the Huncote Railway as it approached the bridge over the Thurlestone Brook, mid-way on its journey to Narborough.

A wonderfully atmospheric quarry scene once so typical of the 1950s. A four wheeled 'puggie', Peckett No.1668 of 1928, hauls her load of dumb buffered side door wagons to the crusher. Collection D.W. Webb; C.E. Manger.

7. ENDERBY QUARRY

The Nuneaton to Hinkley section of the Trent Valley Railway, between Birmingham and Leicester, received the Royal Assent on 13th August 1859. The first sod was turned by Lord Curzon on 19th October 1859 and the combined line was to become The South Leicester Railway. The contractor was Messrs Brassey & Fields who completed the short section between Nuneaton and Hinkley in 1862, with the remainder of the double track the following year. The line was absorbed into the LNWR and became a part of the LMS in 1923. Narborough Station opened 1st January 1864 and had originally boasted two signal boxes, one at the end of the up platform, the other on the down side at the western end. This box controlled the goods yard and the Enderby branch junction and exchange sidings.

The Enderby branch was jointly controlled by the London and North Western and Midland Railways as a single track mineral only branch of some two and a half miles, terminating at the Enderby quarries. A Private Siding Agreement (PSA) was drawn up between the joint railway companies committee and G.W. & A.F. Rawson and the Enderby Granite Company, dated 17th July 1890. Other agreements

between the Joint Committee included provision of telegraph poles and wires along the branch, dated 6th March, 1903. The Narborough & Enderby Granite Co. required a siding at the junction of the branch line and in March 1896 agreed to pay 3d a ton on all traffic over and above the rates operating to and from the LNWR Narborough station.

The Enderby Granite Co. had agreed with the joint railway to erect and maintain, at their expense, a screen over the branch line to catch any material that might fall from the Company's aerial ropeway, between Narborough and Red Hill Quarries.

Locomotives regularly working the Enderby branch were Midland 3F 0-6-0s, built by Johnson from 1875 and found on most of the former MR system. They were allocated to Leicester shed and worked from Humberstone Road yard, their duties including the shunting of stone traffic at Croft Quarry as well as that at Narborough where an early afternoon trip ran up the Enderby branch. With increasingly heavy traffic and larger wagon loads, the 3Fs were found wanting for brakes so more powerful locos appeared over the years, culminating perhaps in the comparatively gigantic BR class 9F 2-10-0s. The Enderby branch left the

main line to the west of Narborough station, connecting with four exchange sidings and one long head shunt. A wide curve through 90 degrees passed over the Fosse Way near Langham Bridge on the river Soar, the line rising on a gently graded embankment. This road latterly became the busy A46 Leicester to Coventry road, the original narrow brick single arch bridge causing a bottle neck as motor traffic gradually increased. This bridge was replaced in 1959 by a wider single span steel girder bridge, the old 'A' road now relegated to the B4114. The line then continued on a straight course, passing over the Huncote Road where a long loop siding with exchange platform served the Huncote, Narborough and Red Hill quarries. The aerial ropeway, mentioned earlier, passed overhead. This loop siding had catch points at both ends. Further on the minor road, Forest Lane, passed under the railway, where a turnout on the east side connected with two sidings of 120 yards or so. These in turn served a spur branch nearly 500 yards long, to the Enderby Brick Works where there was a large Hoffman kiln.

The spur was known as the 'Asylum Siding' from about 1916 as it served a nearby County Hospital. From here the line, still rising, ran through a cutting

DORIS outside the Enderby Quarry crushing plant in 1955. Her deep timber dumb buffers cope with the varying types of quarry wagons. M. Mason.

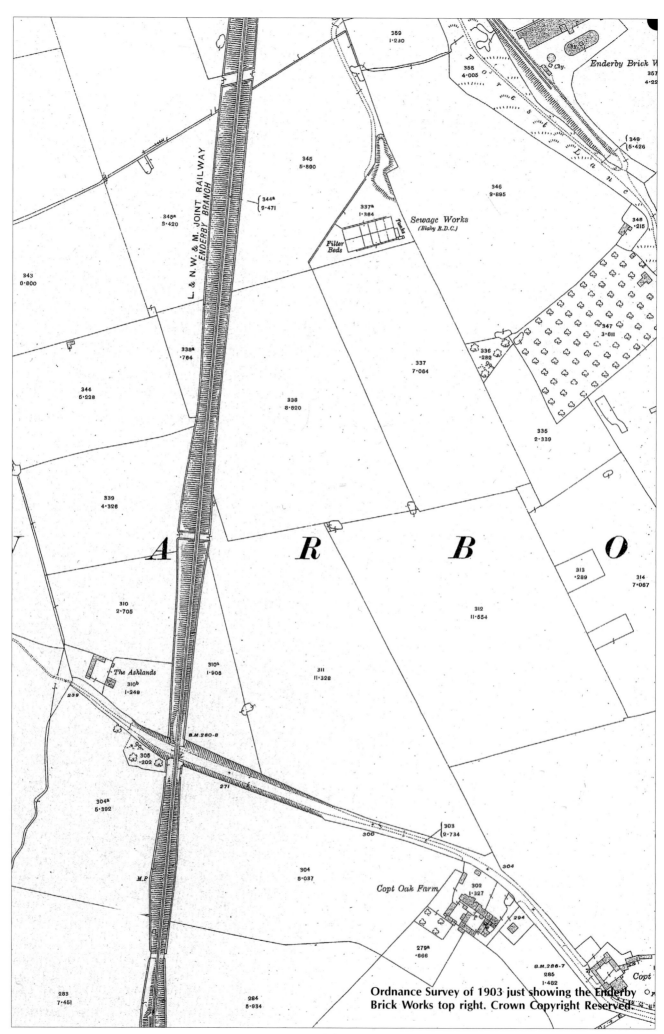

Ordnance Survey of 1903 just showing the Enderby Brick Works top right. Crown Copyright Reserved

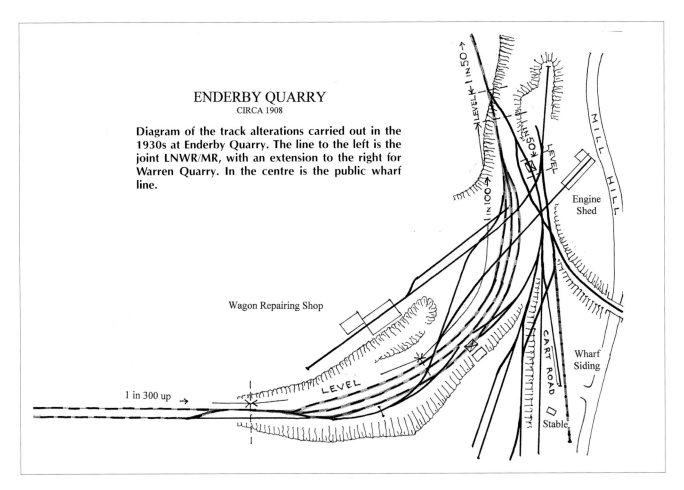

ENDERBY QUARRY
CIRCA 1908

Diagram of the track alterations carried out in the 1930s at Enderby Quarry. The line to the left is the joint LNWR/MR, with an extension to the right for Warren Quarry. In the centre is the public wharf line.

with Seine Lane passing over the single track. At this point the single track became two as the line approached Enderby Quarries; on the right-hand side there were spoil tips. The line then curved sharply to the west in three sidings; these had been put in during 1908-9, replacing a former simple track arrangement. A reverse spur served an engine shed. From a short head shunt the line joined a 'Y' junction, with one branch to the west on an embankment terminating at Seigwart's Fireproof Floor Works. The second arm of the 'Y' junction continued east, terminating in four sidings beneath the stone crushing plant and loading out facility. The other arm of the junction turned north-east, crossing over Mill Hill Lane by an over bridge and ran for half a mile at the base of the hill occupied by 'The Park'. Passing under Harold's Lane at The Warren, the branch then entered the Warren Quarry and split into seven sidings. A short siding opposite the engine shed spur, had a run-through wagon repair workshop. The Granite Company had constructed the bridge over Mill Hill Lane at its own cost, along with the sidings eastward to the Warren Quarry.

The two railway companies, the LNW and MR were entitled to build on quarry land and enjoyed free access to the sidings, certainly as far as Mill Hill Lane. The rest of the working was left to the quarry locomotives. On 10th August 1908 an agreement was made between the Enderby & Stoney Stanton Granite Co Ltd. and the Midland and LNW to

extend the Enderby branch Railway. The railway companies built and maintained additional sidings on land previously owned by the Granite Co., at a nominal rent of 10/- per annum. The Granite Co. was 'to provide all the materials required', and their locomotives were 'to place the loaded railway wagons so that they could be readily reached by the Railway Companies engines'.

Several stone quarries grew up at Enderby over the years, with the owning Marston, Rawson and Freer families prominent. A small quarry between Kirk Lane and Coalpit Lane (later Blaby Road), to the east of the village, had no rail access. Early maps dating from 1825 show quarries but it was not until these families became involved that they developed beyond just local Parish needs. The Enderby Hall Estate was sold in 1865 and this included a 'Granite Stone Quarry'.

In 1881 there were quarries owned by George Marston, with his manager Henry Grace. There were other quarry owners and there was a further quarrying partnership, Nowell & Robson. By 1895 brothers George William Rawson and Alfred Freer Rawson traded as Rawson & Rawson, having extensive quarries employing 300 men.

In 1890 the first of two new Hunslet steam locomotives was delivered to Enderby Quarry; this was No.476 TROT, an 0-4-0ST. It was scrapped in 1950 after sixty years of service. The second engine, No.553, was delivered three years later and this too took the

name TROT, its predecessor being renamed JESSIE. This second loco was scrapped in 1937. The third new loco was a Peckett 0-4-0ST, No.1759 ELIZABETH of 1928. This was transferred to Mountsorrel in November 1957. Another Peckett had been acquired in June 1913, second-hand from John Lysaght Ltd. of Newport; this was works number 801 built in 1899 and named GWEN. She was scrapped in 1934. THE EARL, another Hunslet, No.669 of 1898, was transferred from Stoney Stanton but returned there in 1948. THE COUNTESS, named after the wife of the said Earl was transferred from Mountsorrel in 1944 and then sent to Stoney Stanton. GERALD, the same class of engine and built in 1907, came from Stoney Stanton in 1950 and was scrapped two years later. CORNWALL, yet another 0-4-0ST, broke the trend of manufacturers, as it was built by Andrew Barclay, No.1386 and came on hire from Abelson & Co (Engineers) Ltd of Birmingham in February 1952. It remained for only a month or two. No.1668 DORIS of 1928, another Peckett, came from Mountsorrel in 1953 and met her end in November 1958. THE CHAIRMAN, a four wheeled diesel mechanical loco built by Ruston Hornsby to works number 23791, was built in 1946 and had been at Stoney Stanton for its first ten years. After only two years at Enderby, this loco was moved to Mountsorrel but returned to Enderby in 1971, to be scrapped in February 1981. BUNTY was the last loco, an 0-4-0 diesel mechanical, No.4210018

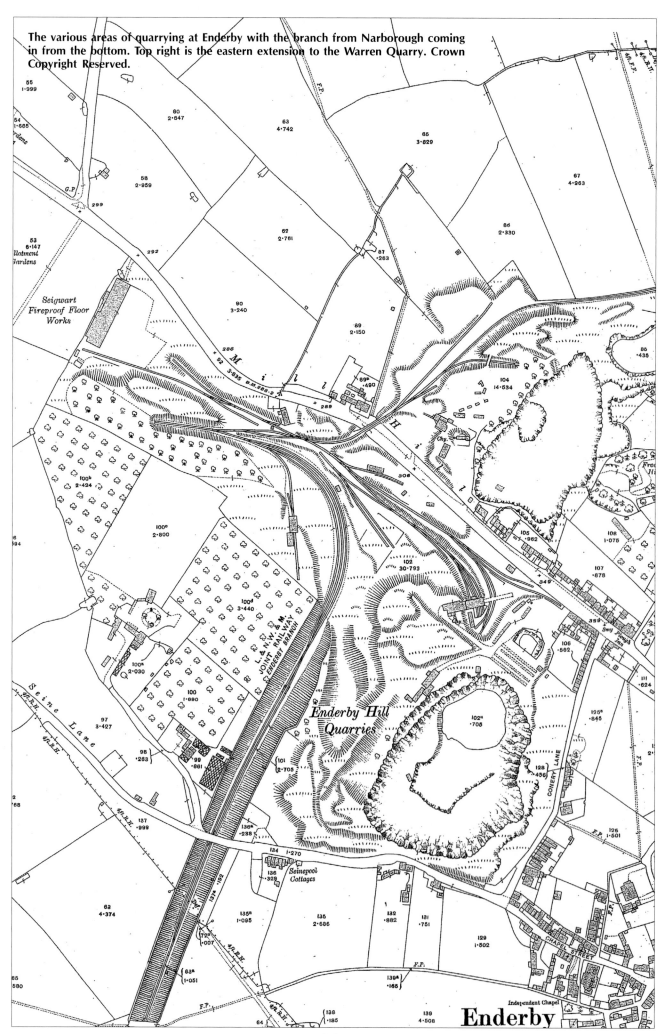

The various areas of quarrying at Enderby with the branch from Narborough coming in from the bottom. Top right is the eastern extension to the Warren Quarry. Crown Copyright Reserved.

Seigwart Fireproof Floor Works

Seine Lane

L. & N.W. & M. JOINT RAILWAY ENDERBY BRANCH

Enderby Hill Quarries

Seinepool Cottages

CONERY LANE

CHAPEL STREET

Independent Chapel

Enderby

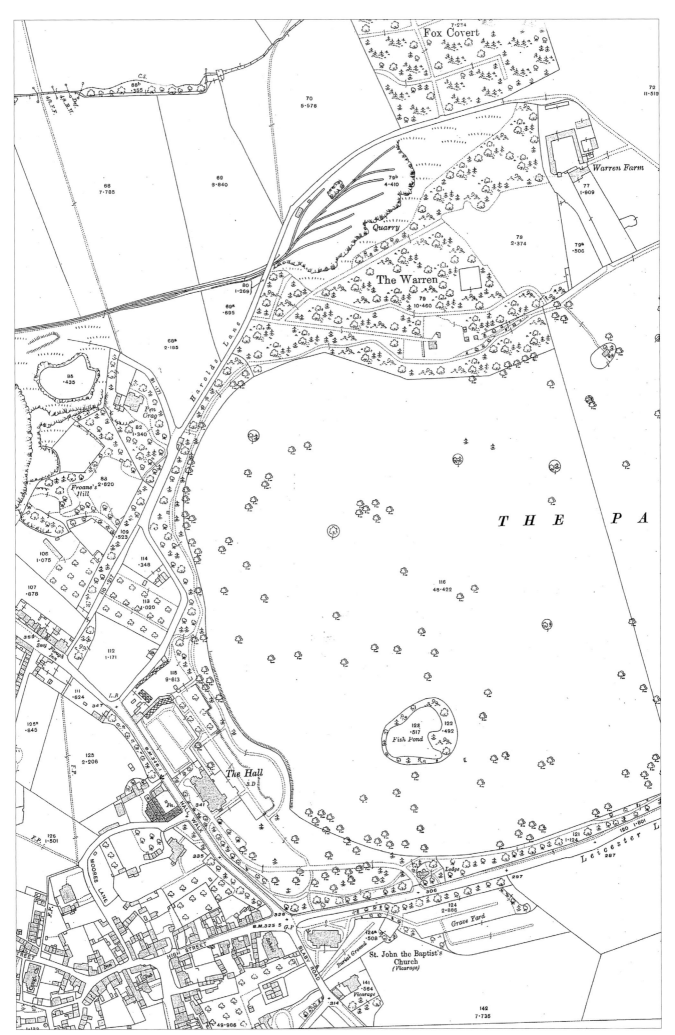

Fox Covert

Warren Farm

Quarry

The Warren

Pen Crag

Froane's Hill

T H E   P A

Fish Pond

The Hall

Lodge

Leicester L

Grave Yard

St. John the Baptist's
Church
(Vicarage)

Vicarage

HIGH STREET

MOORES LANE

BLABY ROAD

DORIS was a Peckett, No.1668 built in 1928 and sadly scrapped in November 1958. She had been transferred from the Mountsorrel Quarry in 1953 to Enderby where she saw out the rest of her days. Andrew Moore collection, courtesy Kevin Lane.

built by John Fowler in 1950 and rebuilt in 1964/5 by Thomas Hill. Renumbered 146C, it came from Stoney Stanton in 1958 and remained at Enderby until February 1976, when it was transferred to Mountsorrel Quarry. It worked at the Barrow-on-Soar stone loading out terminal.

At least sixty open wagons were ordered from the Gloucester Wagon Company about the time that the first locomotive for Enderby came, in 1890. These were three plank opens built on a steel solebar, with a tare of 4 tons 9 cwt and a capacity of ten tons, with split spoke wheels and brakes (wooden blocks) to one side only; unusually, they had five link couplings. Ironwork was black with the body painted in a Midland Railway deep maroon, with white block letters reading ENDERBY GRANITE QUARRIES with a wagon number. The sides were fixed and the ends had supporting wood stanchions, suggesting that they were loaded and unloaded by hand.

A further fleet of open wagons with three planks was delivered. The capacity remained at 10 tons but with a tare of 5 tons 7 cwt. These had central drop down doors to both sides but were numbered on the end panels. The livery was dark red-brown, including solebars and were sign-written THE ENDERBY & STONEY

STANTON GRANITE Co. in white block letters, shaded black to the right side and below. Another series of wagons had a capacity of 13 tons and a tare of 6 tons 14 cwt. Two heavy end stanchions supported a half rounded end to the six planks. Lettering was similar but included the wagon number to the left bottom side with 'Limited' abbreviated to Ltd. For internal use, the Enderby quarry used small timber contractor type wagons with four fixed planks to one side, the other side had a single deep plank with drop down door. These were still in use in the mid-1950s, along with a few steel wagons of similar design.

A narrow gauge network operated within the close confines of the working faces, the track feeding the crushing plant and removing spoil to tips. The gauge was 2ft and all four locomotives were sent to Earl Shilton Quarry when no longer required. The narrow gauge locos were the 'four generals' by-now familiar from earlier notes: BOBS, LESTER, BULLER and KITCHENER.

The quarry to the north-east of Mill Hill road backed onto Froans's Hill and was the site of this narrow gauge railway. The crushing plant was nearest to the Warren Quarry standard gauge railway which at this point had two short sidings into the area, with one longer siding to spoil tips. A double track

incline led down into the deepest area of stone quarrying and this and the radiating sidings out from its base were still in-situ in 1950, and this was after some forty years of not having been in use! These tracks were finally retrieved for scrap in the late 1950s.

Enderby Quarry closed operations in 1979/80, with a subsidiary of Redland Aggregates, Redland Purle, backfilling some quarried areas. Today the site of the main works has been made into an industrial estate, thus obliterating most signs of this former heavy activity. The local council has made excellent use of the old track formation of the Enderby branch, for this is now a pleasant public footpath passing through woodland which almost obscures the long concrete transfer platform for the Huncote Railway. Bridges still span roads which lead into the Narborough residential estate.

The modern world came to Enderby's railway when Fowler diesel BUNTY arrived, from Stoney Stanton Quarries, in 1958. Collection Andrew Moore.

An almost timeless quarry scene at Enderby in 1910, a steam loco busy amongst scattered piles of prepared stone setts. Collection Andrew Moore.

The Enderby crushing and rail loading out plant, with the old engine shed on the left, with all the signs of rail traffic having ceased in May 1974, a rather sad scene never to be repeated. Sydney A. Leleux.

Four plank private owner wagon No.404 in 1954, when it was 'internal use only'. It has recently been renovated with new top planks. David W. Webb.

A scene of confusion, except to a quarry man, in 1970. Collection Andrew Moore.

An 'O' gauge model of wagon No.527, which had a capacity of 13 tons, built by David Webb. The livery is red with white letters and black shading. David W. Webb.

Peckett 0-4-0ST ELIZABETH, looking the worse for wear, outside the engine shed at Enderby Quarry. Inside lurks the diesel BUNTY. David W. Webb.

An old photograph of 1876, of the early stages of extraction at Enderby. Some thirty men are clearing the overburden.